SOUTHWESTERN INDIAN BRACELETS

The Essential Cuff

Paula A. Baxter
Photography by Barry Katzen

Schiffer Publishing Ltd

4880 Lower Valley Road • Atglen, PA 19310

Other Schiffer Books by the Author:
Southwest Silver Jewelry: The First Century, 978-0-7643-1244-1
Southwestern Indian Rings, 978-0-7643-3875-5

Other Schiffer Books on Related Subjects:
Fred Harvey Jewelry: 1900–1955, 978-0-7643-4448-0
Navajo Silversmith Fred Peshlakai: His Life & Art,
978-0-7643-4745-0
*Reassessing Hallmarks of Native Southwest Jewelry: Artists, Traders,
Guilds, and the Government*, 978-0-7643-4670-5

Designed by Molly Shields
Type set in HoratioDLig/Adobe Garamond (T1)

Cover image: Bracelet with silver repoussé and square-cut coral
set in double bezel by Delbert Gordon, c. 2010. Courtesy of
Territorial Indian Arts.

ISBN: 978-0-7643-4868-6
Printed in China

Published by Schiffer Publishing, Ltd.
4880 Lower Valley Road
Atglen, PA 19310
Phone: (610) 593-1777; Fax: (610) 593-2002
E-mail: Info@schifferbooks.com

For our complete selection of fine books on this and related
subjects, please visit our website at www.schifferbooks.com. You
may also write for a free catalog.

This book may be purchased from the publisher. Please try your
bookstore first.

We are always looking for people to write books on new and
related subjects. If you have an idea for a book, please contact us
at proposals@schifferbooks.com.

Schiffer Publishing's titles are available at special discounts for
bulk purchases for sales promotions or premiums. Special editions,
including personalized covers, corporate imprints, and excerpts
can be created in large quantities for special needs. For more
information, contact the publisher.

DEDICATION

This book is dedicated to Orville Tsinnie,
the friend who makes my bracelets.

CONTENTS

ACKNOWLEDGMENTS

A design history of this nature requires many contributors, and their assistance has been invaluable. The economic reality of producing a book like this means the author must rely on the help of individuals to depict a living art. Museum photography, however, provides a benchmark for quality examples, and I am grateful to Deborah Slaney at the Albuquerque Museum for the use of two images from their permanent collection. Thanks also to Diana Pardue, Curator of Collections, and the Library staff at the Heard Museum for the use of their archival files.

We wish to thank the following contributors whose bracelets adorn this book: Laura Anderson; Philip Bacon; Robert Bauver; Joan Caballero; Steve and Mary Delzio, The Mexican Shack; Stuart Early; Eason Eige; Faust Gallery; Abby Kent Flythe; the Funny Company, Japan; Janie Kasarjian; Michael Horsley; Ingrid Levine; Alston and Deborah Neal; Allan and Joyce Niederman; Paul and Valerie Piazza; Norman L. Sandfield; Douglas and Kris Sill; Karen Sires; Martha Hopkins Struever; Vicki Turbeville; Erick Van Itallie; Gene, Mike, and Lisa Waddell; Ken Wolf; and those collectors who wished their holdings to remain as Private Collection.

Others who need to be thanked are: Christel Bieri; Ernie Bulow; Laura Cardinal and Bruce McGee, Heard Museum Shop; Dexter Cirillo; Bill Faust; Marney Field; Warren Fischbach; Robert Gallegos; John Hill; Charles King; Dr. Henrietta Lidchi; Danny Luwe; Ruth Ellen Saarinen; Barry and Steve Simpson.

Then, there are the artists: those who came before, those who are working currently, and those who will continue making this fine art. This book is meant for you, but I'd like to express my gratitude to some individuals in particular. Many thanks to Veronica and Dylan Poblano, Mike and Allison Bird-Romero, the Gaussoin family, Jimmie Harrison, Ernie Lister, Chris and Luwanna Nieto, Chris and Pat Pruitt, and the incomparable Liz Wallace. This also includes my Facebook friends, who are often on the road and always (like me) wishing we were in Gallup—preferably at Earl's.

Back East, I'd like to thank Nancy Schiffer and her team, Dr. Ralph Peters and the students of Berkeley College Westchester, New York and Online, Dr. Mark Kupersmith, Dr. Judith Kornberg, Sandra Carpenter and Charlie Morrow, Daniel Fermon, and Daniel Starr. My deepest gratitude goes to my husband Barry Katzen, along with the rescue rabbits who serve as a dedicated audience and daily joy. Any errors in this text are strictly my own.

Paula A. Baxter
White Plains, New York

INTRODUCTION

Making the Essential Cuff

We are all connected in our love of beauty. Bracelets created by the Indians of the American Southwest are prized because they are beautiful and make their wearers look and feel good. Like rings, they can signify prosperity, status, and taste. As adornment, they also represent a vital living art. This book is the story of how these bracelets came to be meaningful and popular and how they remain so today.

The design history of the Southwestern Indian bracelet is a narrative with psychological and sociological overtones. These examples of beauty have moved far beyond being wristguards and Native hard goods. They're now chosen for their materials, motifs, and cuff shape—and the way that they visually enhance the people who wear them.

Anthropological investigation created a framework for the beginning of their story. Add to this tale how the processes of acculturation, popular culture, and profound respect for aesthetic harmony fashioned the bracelet into the most passionately collected of all Southwestern souvenirs; in fact, the period leading up to 1980 elevated this jewelry form into something much more substantial than originally intended. The result is an account of enduring Native American ingenuity.

What makes this narrative even more relevant is that it's being written at a time when the nature of the young twenty-first century is being shaped by economic adversity. Jewelry, an enjoyable example of current material culture, is proving to be essential to our souls. Native peoples who experienced hardship in the aftermath of the Civil War, Anglo American settler expansion, and the Great Depression, fabricated creative adornment even in the bleakest of times. They did this so well and so continuously that their jewelry design has proven classic in nature.

Contemporary and future mainstream jewelry innovations remain influenced by Native Style. Back in the 1970s, rising fashion designer Ralph Lauren foresaw the timeless allure of Southwestern metal and stone jewelry that still resided at the center of a thriving ethnic arts market. More than ever, Native arts form a bridge between cultures that have no other recourse than to grow demonstrably more connected. Whether featured on QVC's home shopping channel or seen in the pages of *O, The Oprah Magazine*, Southwestern Indian bracelets are part of today's jewelry design history.

The cuff itself has an impressive historical pedigree. Bracelets in this shape were made and worn by the ancient Egyptians; they appear on tomb wall paintings, and graced the wrists of pharaohs and high officials. Cuffs also were worn by early cultures in Africa and China. Even the Romans adopted the form as part of ceremonial dress. In the New World, varied examples of these bracelet shapes have been found in the ruined cities of the Mayan and Incan empires.

Cuffs were revived over the centuries. Large cuffs were considered bold and masculine. In the early twentieth century, however, jewelry and fashion designers appropriated them for feminine wear. In the 1930s, the jewelry designer Verdura created a Maltese Cross cuff for wear with outfits by Coco Chanel. No wonder that Southwestern Indian cuffs, especially those that looked midcentury modern, achieved general popularity around this time. The cuff had become an iconic form.

This book traces the reasons for this iconic stature. We can track ongoing craft innovation, social change, and the impact of popular culture on individual artists. Along the way, we learn significant details about jewelry history and American enterprise. Native Americans have *always* made essential contributions to design.

Chapter 1 examines sources for designs and how styles came into being. The second and third chapters look at historic bracelets, the foundation for traditional styles. Chapter 4 details how the curio bracelet impacted current and future work. In Chapter 5, we see that between 1930 and 1950 Native smiths made bracelets in what became considered the classic style, which would become old-style in later decades when artists sought to pay tribute to an earlier era. Chapter 6 looks at the powerful social forces of the 1970s, the publishing explosion on the topic, and how Navajo silverwork came to represent all Native design, while Chapter 7 celebrates post-1980 talent, persistence, and the continuity of Native Style. Chapter 8 discusses the demand for finely designed Southwestern Indian bracelets in this age of Internet auctions and globalization.

Shaping the Southwestern Indian Bracelet

When the time came for making jewelry from metal, Indian smiths turned unerringly to a jewelry form that was easy to shape and comfortable to wear. The earliest reports on Native jewelry-making were created by non-Natives from an ethnographical viewpoint. Since metalworking was a new craft,

Sixteen-year-old Rita Neal commissioned this silver cuff with spider in 1932. Courtesy of Territorial Indian Arts.

Four early twentieth-century wristguards, or ketohs, with chisel and stamp work. Courtesy of Philip Bacon Collection.

anthropologists were most interested in its transmission between tribes of the region. Much of this reporting was done at a time when it was expected that Indian cultures would be absorbed and destroyed. Seeking to document poten-

tially vanishing Indian arts, nineteenth-century anthropological studies focused mainly on reproducing images from historic indigenous utilitarian crafts: pottery, weaving, and carving from stone or wood.

Southwestern tribes obtained metal ornaments through trade with Plains Indians and Hispanic colonists as early as the eighteenth century. Natives initially made their adornment from materials other than metal, and contemporary

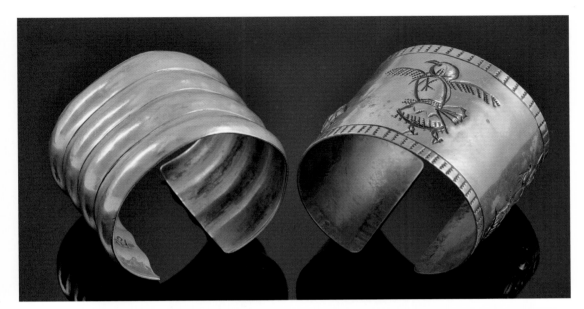

Two brass cuffs by Felix Chama, Santo Domingo Pueblo, 1975; these bracelets resemble the early efforts of smiths who usually work in brass and copper before silver. Courtesy of Joan Caballero.

This early twentieth-century cuff shows a blacksmith's approach in the way it is hand hammered, with unique construction techniques where long sides of rectangular settings bar are chiseled into place. Courtesy of Philip Bacon Collection.

Three silver cuffs with repoussé and peyote bud center; each has the same stamps arranged in different ways, c. 2007, by Edison Smith. Courtesy of Eason Eige Collection, Albuquerque, NM.

Silver bracelet by master smith McKee Platero, c. 2004. Courtesy of Janie Kasarjian Collection.

Two silver bands with elaborate stamps; one bracelet might have been made for a monogram, 1920–1930s. Courtesy of Philip Bacon Collection.

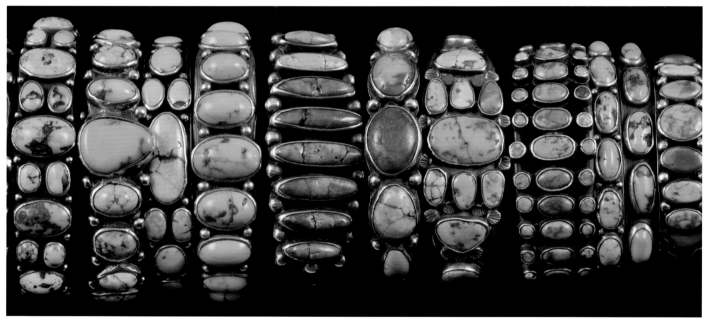

Multiple turquoise stone row bracelets, an early twentieth-century emerging style. Courtesy of Philip Bacon Collection.

Pueblo artists still create shell bracelets that look much like those fashioned by their ancestors. The early to mid-nineteenth century contact with itinerant Mexican ironworkers and incoming European American soldiers and settlers made learning the practical craft of blacksmithing a priority.

The Navajo turned to metalworking in earnest after 1868, when they returned from internment at the Bosque Redondo. Always a mobile people, Navajo smiths instructed other smiths in jewelry formation at various pueblos over the next three decades. This extensive transmission of the craft was learned

from Native informants in the 1930s, many with living memories of the first smiths (Adair, 14). Silvercraft in the Rio Grande and western pueblos was stimulated by Mexican and Anglo settlers and visiting Navajo smiths. The physical appearance of earrings, bracelets, rings, manta pins, and belts from this early start

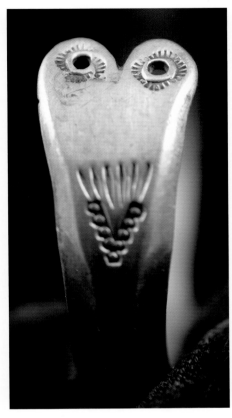

Detail of carinated cuff with double end terminals pierced with holes, simple chisel decoration, early twentieth century. Courtesy of Steve and Mary Delzio, The Mexican Shack.

Cuff with center turquoise stone on disk bought and worn by artist Max Ernst during his time in Sedona, Arizona, 1939. Private Collection.

time were similar, yet subtle differences marked Navajo versus Pueblo metal decoration on adornment.

This First Phase, as non-Natives would label it, ran from 1868 to 1900. The first non-Natives to study early metalworking marveled at bracelets that were richly decorated despite the use of simple, rough tools. Silver bands could be shaped on a mandrel and hammered to completion. Handmade dies and punches created decorative patterns. The first Native smiths fashioned designs that grew in sophistication as their confidence increased with experience.

Indian smiths started by learning to work iron, brass, and copper—just as many new jewelers do today. Silver,

Two bracelets from 1930s–1940s: an early cluster cuff and a single stone band. Courtesy of Michael Horsley.

Wide silver cuff set with Morenci turquoise by Joe H. Quintana, Cochiti Pueblo, 1940s–1950s. Private Collection.

however, quickly became the material of choice and Natives craved adornment made from the "metal of the moon." The early silversmiths chased, hammered, gouged, and incised decorative lines and patterns on silver. They used local sandstone, or tufa, to make molds for casting. In the 1880s stones were added, usually garnets, drilled beads, or pieces of crudely cut and polished turquoise. Enthusiastic non-Native Indian traders saw the possibilities in this new adornment; they found ways of obtaining polished stones and better tools to aid Indian jewelry-makers.

By the start of the twentieth century, the results were very promising indeed. Between 1900 and 1930, Indian-made bracelets were created in a dual stream: bracelets for Native consumption became more physically attractive through the use of stones and strong designs, while a more generic brand of bracelet was shaped for the tourist market. Certain distinctive elements appeared in each group. Over time, they became so recognizable that observers were commenting about the "traditional" and "classic" look of such adornment. Good work for a craft that was barely sixty years old!

Because Indian jewelry quickly became popular with non-Natives, collectors demanded "authentic" Native-worn pieces, probably in reaction to the growth of commercial adornment. This

established two simultaneous markets for Indian jewelry, including bracelets. One market favored commercially made and curio-type designs in lightweight styles attractive to tourists. The other stream advanced Native jewelry designs that were not commercially inspired.

When those selling Southwestern Indian jewelry introduced such labels as "traditional" style and "classic" style, they did so in the hope of separating the Native-inspired jewelry design from the commercial designs. These purveyors were eager to place "traditional" and "classic" labels on this work, even though the styles themselves were far from old. Between 1900 and 1950, certain decorative motifs and designs emerged that could realistically be called classic. Bracelets created after 1930 reflected improved craft techniques and more sophisticated construction, which made the cuffs all the more desirable to buyers.

After 1930, Southwestern Indian bracelet cuffs gained new stature from a growing trend: the rise of the named individual artist. Native smiths were encouraged to create hallmarks or otherwise sign their creations. This development was a concession to Anglo interests, but it led to a much more important transformation; individuals began to shed their artisan status—they were *artists* in the full sense of the word. During the 1960s and 1970s, master innovators with names like Begay, Loloma, Lovato, and Quintana moved into the forefront of the ethnic marketplace.

Bracelets attracted collectors who became patrons. Cuffs could be worn by

This tufa cast silver bracelet is classic in its curves and symmetry, c. 1950. Courtesy of Joan Caballero.

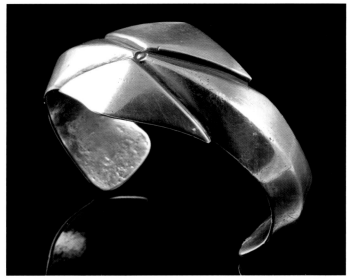

Turquoise bracelet that was pictured on inside cover of May 1951 Arizona Highways; note heart design on end of row stones. Private Collection.

A silver cuff with a "midcentury modern" aesthetic feel. Courtesy of Abby Kent Flythe.

Unusual raised silver bracelet and pin, made with turquoise, shell, and abalone, attributed to Oliver Cellicion of Zuni, mid-twentieth century. Courtesy of Andrew Muñana Collection.

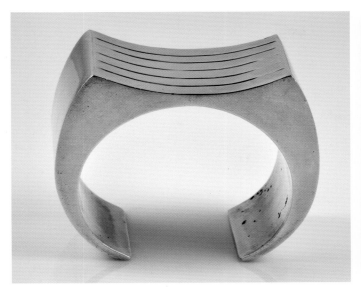

All-silver grooved cuff by Chester Nez, a former Navajo Code Talker, 1960s–1970s. Courtesy of Doug and Kris Sill Collection.

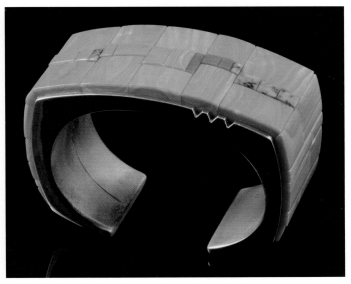

A bracelet with peach coral and Morenci turquoise by Richard Chavez, San Felipe Pueblo, 2012. Courtesy of Erik Van Itallie.

Master jeweler Charles Loloma made this 14K gold bracelet set with four rows of Mikimoto pearls, 1970s. Private Collection.

Silver grooved cuff with natural turquoise and onyx by Preston Monongye, 1960s. Courtesy of Waddell Trading Company.

both men and women. Non-Indian men in early twentieth-century America weren't quick to add bracelets to their wardrobe on basic gender grounds, but a masculine cuff was allowable. By the 1960s, Native-made cuff wristwatches and watchband bracelets caught men's interest. Femininely shaped cuffs sold well to women, who were taking over dominance in the fashion marketplace. A number of these new collectors didn't shy away from strongly designed wrist wear. Native master artist Charles Loloma proved to be an unusually adept salesman, setting a precedent for jewelers who admired his technical and verbal skills.

Designing the Bracelet

This design history of the Southwestern Indian bracelet parallels the narrative of the author's *Southwestern Indian Rings*. The present book, therefore, features the elements of maker craft, culture, and individualist endeavor that are most important to understanding bracelet creation. Just as the Indian-made ring could be souvenir or art, bracelets were commercial or classy. Bracelets possessed a certain added cachet, however, and earned their makers more money than rings. From the beginning, bracelet designs embodied spirit and elegance.

This visual distinctiveness sprang in part from Native enjoyment in embracing the craft of metalsmithing. This book largely focuses on the period from the start of metal jewelry-making up to 1980. The years since 1980 have been a time of consolidation for individualist artistry. Contemporary bracelet-making draws on a repertoire of decoration and design that was created between 1868 and 1980. When we evaluate the history of design over these years, a pattern of ingenuity emerges. While anthropologists speak of florescence and art historians map the influence of patronage, the evidence shows that Native jewelers have always been in control of their designs.

One of the most aggravating misnomers about Indian design has been the popular culture perception by non-Indians that every decorative motif on Native-made art has a symbolic meaning. Over the years, the author has attended Indian arts shows where invariably one or more earnest consumers plead with artists to tell them what their design

A classic style five-stone Lone Mountain Navajo row bracelet by Fred Peshlakai, 1950s–1960s. Courtesy of Waddell Trading Company.

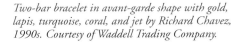

Two-bar bracelet in avant-garde shape with gold, lapis, turquoise, coral, and jet by Richard Chavez, 1990s. Courtesy of Waddell Trading Company.

Lightweight Navajo tourist-era child's bracelet with popular leaves, turquoise and branch coral stones, probably made by a member of the Tahe family, c. 1960s. Courtesy of Norman L. Sandfield.

This gold and Lone Mountain cuff by Lee Yazzie is typical of contemporary high-end design, 1980–1981. Courtesy of Ingrid Levine.

Silver avant-garde shaped, hand-cut cuff by Isaiah Ortiz, San Felipe Pueblo, c. 2010. Courtesy of Norman L. Sandfield.

"means." This assumption dates back to the first decade of the twentieth century, when non-Indian middlemen sought to make mass-produced Indian jewelry and arts more interesting and saleable by inventing charts of "Indian symbols." Curio work was invested in these motifs. Chapter 1 provides an overview of Native design sources that extend to stories, beliefs, places, colors, and materials possessing spiritual qualities.

Providing symbolical features for designs has been accepted by Native artists to a certain extent. Many find it easier to go along with this cultural neediness on the part of consumers in the hope that it will aid sales. On the other hand, jewelers can incorporate a genuine spiritual aspect into their design or construction, e.g., a Navajo silversmith who chooses to make four split shanks on rings and bracelets because this number has sacred meaning in his or her culture. The finest Native artists

Cast watchband from 1950s to 1960s with modern watch added. Courtesy of Allan and Joyce Niederman Collection.

Cornrow beads on a silver cuff with hallmark "LC," post-1980. Courtesy of Allan and Joyce Niederman Collection.

render designs with some aspect of their cultural beliefs embedded in their creations. Master jewelers are brilliant at such aesthetic cultural references; they use high-quality materials to produce an art work with Native feeling and contemporary bravura.

Early anthropologists and collectors, from James and Matilda Stevenson to George Gustaf Heye, promoted utilitarian Indian crafts and promoted them as decorative art objects. The Fred Harvey Company continued this interest in decorative display; Navajo weavings originally intended for wear or for floor coverings were hung on walls like painting canvases on exhibit. This kind of showcase presentation would come later in the early twentieth century for Southwestern Indian silverwork. The ongoing commercialization of metalwork might have diminished the scholarly appeal of silver jewelry, but once museums began

exhibiting this adornment, bracelets with sculptural tendencies stood out.

In the meantime, Native artisans, not yet named artists, were not as passive as non-Native narratives of the times suggest. Artists adopted and adapted design motifs that suited their aesthetic sense or group identity. Sometimes attribution of designs to specific families or individuals, as at Zuni Pueblo, proved erroneous because Native concepts of intellectual property were more elastic than non-Natives expected. The problem surfaced again in the mid-twentieth century, when Indian traders attempted to create a vogue for tribal styles that were based on a prevailing technique, such as overlay. In reality, tribes happily copied each other's designs, showing the pitfalls in such labeling. Nor did such labels account for collaborations. When jewelry, including bracelets, might have the silver hand-wrought by a Navajo and

the stones set by a Pueblo Indian, whose design was prevailing or dominant?

If we concentrate our observation on the historic, vintage, and modern artistic periods of bracelet design, and how each group evolved from its predecessors, certain visual patterns materialize. Surface patterning serves as a significant indicator of aesthetic development. Abstract and geometric decoration marks First Phase creations. The historic first decades of the twentieth century saw an integration of stronger geometric patterns and the start of figural designs. In the decades after 1930, designs show greater experimentation in tune with the increasing modernization of Southwestern Native life—factors such as electrification, radio, improved roads, and better tools combined to make metalworking easier and training more available. More Indians received instruction in this craft at schools and colleges,

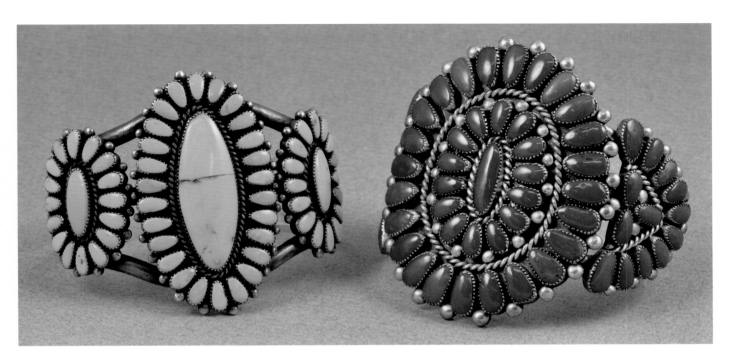

Two classic cluster bracelets by Alice Quam, Zuni: (l.) Villa Grove turquoise, 1940s; (r.) coral, 1960s. Courtesy of Vicki Turbeville.

Unsigned cluster cuff with Blue Gem turquoise, previously owned by Teal McKibben, 1940s–1960s. Courtesy of Vicki Turbeville.

and these artists enjoyed the challenges of incorporating non-traditional metal-working techniques into their work. The American social landscape of the 1960s and 1970s further encouraged individualist endeavor.

A genuine legacy of design inspiration already existed when Indian jewelry-making changed from craft to art. New artists could draw freely from this legacy. What truly helped was that the aesthetic wellspring Native jewelers tapped into had grown out of early Modernism. Natives chose decorative motifs with similarities to those used by Europeans and European Americans. Whether they were organic designs using dragonflies and waterspouts or geometric frets on a rectangular background, the effects were consonant with artistic experimentation of the times. This meant that the design differences between a Mondrian canvas and a Navajo cuff were not very far apart. A closer look at "classic" bracelets made in this period shows us why older Native design has become so renowned.

Wearing the Bracelet

More than any other existing jewelry form, Southwestern Indian-made bracelets are immediately recognized as cuff shaped. While Indian artists do create soldered round bangles or link bracelets on occasion, those who look for a *real* Indian bracelet expect a cuff. The Indian bracelet encircles the wrist—but not completely. Newcomers, if they are lucky, are shown how to put on such a bracelet. The cuff is placed against the inside center of a wrist at an angle, and then rolled over the bone at the side of the wrist.

The bracelet should fit firmly and comfortably. It must lie anchored on the wrist and cannot be shaken out of place. If the circumference of the bracelet shank is too tight or too loose, the wearer feels this imbalance at once. You cannot squeeze yourself into a bracelet that's too small, even though you might so this with shoes or clothing. A bracelet cuff that fits too loosely is ungainly and may fall off. Most wearers expect their cuff to fit in a manner that makes the bracelet a flattering frame for their wrist. For those who like more of a good thing, cuffs can easily be stacked along the forearm.

From the beginning, Native smiths crafted cuffs in masculine, feminine, and child-sized proportions. They produced cuffs according to demand. Even when the curio trade started up with non-Native purchasers in mind, cuffs were made in a range of sizes. Jewelry creators understood

Two views of an early micro inlay design bangle by Carl and Irene Clark, 1980s. Private Collection.

Silver and multi-stone inlay Monument Valley storyteller scene by Vernon Haskie, 1995. Courtesy of Paul and Valerie Piazza.

Two 1930s–1940s cuffs with lively stamps. Courtesy of Philip Bacon Collection.

Three bracelets by Cody Sanderson, (l to r): horned repoussé pattern turned into flames on silver cuff, 1999, previously on loan to Autry Museum; cuff made in 2006; star repoussé, 2008. Courtesy of Eason Eige Collection, Albuquerque, New Mexico.

that pieces should correspond to various body types. Historical evidence shows that Indian men and women wanted and wore some bracelets for everyday activities and held back others for ceremonial and social occasions. Among the Navajo, bracelets along with other metal adornment became known as "hard goods." They were a yardstick to an individual's material wealth and standing. Jewelry could be pawned or held as collateral until needed for a specific purpose.

Once traders and commercial middlemen became involved in the Indian jewelry industry, they meddled with the design and creation process. They altered

Gold cuff set with Persian turquoise by master innovator Julian Lovato, Santo Domingo Pueblo, 1970s. Courtesy of Janie Kasarjian Collection.

Bracelet (r.) with Blue Gem turquoise stone by Joe H. Quintana; the other two bracelets are by Cippy Crazyhorse, including an inverted solid silver big cuff done for owner, early 1980s. Courtesy of Joan Caballero.

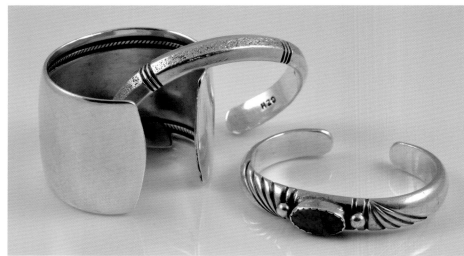

design motifs to what they thought non-Natives would want. One of the largest changes involved making the bracelet (along with other jewelry forms) more lightweight. Non-Natives worried that bracelets made for Native consumption would be thought to be too heavy for regular wear. European American jewelry was generally lightweight; therefore, Indian pieces should be too. While some

tourists became collectors who preferred the feeling of heavier metal pieces, the curio trade embraced bracelets made from sheet silver once it became available.

Over the years, some American Indian jewelers have retained the notion that bracelets for commercial sale shouldn't be massive or heavy. Many Zuni jewelers produce lightweight pieces as a matter of course. Other creators feel that cuffs

should retain some modicum of heft. The solidity of Southwestern Indian bracelets is a characteristic, but not a given, of that essential cuff. Many dealers and collectors particularly cherish the concept of a sculptural bracelet.

In addition, bracelets made by non-Natives living in the American Southwest espouse the cuff shape as one of their product characteristics. Such pieces go

A basket of bracelets. Courtesy of Philip Bacon Collection.

Earl's Restaurant in Gallup, NM, is the favorite destination for every Southwestern Indian artist, dealer, and collector.

by the label "Southwestern Style." Sometimes consumers new to collecting become confused by this distinction. Southwestern Style jewelry can and does resemble Native-made work; those in the know in the marketplace, however, recognize that this term means the pieces are usually not Indian-made but do reflect Native design elements. Looked at in a certain way, this is a compliment to Native ingenuity, since imitation has always been a genuine form of flattery.

Design has certain meanings when related to decorative art objects. When a jewelry form made by a non-Western culture attracts large numbers of buyers and collectors from Western culture, this form's design merits some examination. For example, anthropologists studying Southwestern Indian cultures marveled at the ready Native adoption of the European and Middle Eastern Moorish-inspired *naja* pendant and pomegranate seed beads for necklace decoration from horse gear. Bracelets, however, offer a more complex palette for design tendencies.

A bracelet's **design** can be characterized as an arrangement, or composition, of visual motifs on the constructed piece. A common non-Native misunderstanding associated with Indian jewelry is the assumption that any decoration thereon is significant in terms of the maker's culture. In fact, the collision between Native and European cultures formed a particular kind of artistic collaboration. While it's true that some sources of decorative impulse date back to pre-contact times, others are the product of popular culture. For example, Native jewelers adopted the non-Native Valentine heart motif by the 1920s and 1930s (and possibly earlier, since Victorians loved this shape); as acculturation increased, it became popular all on its own.

Design elements arranged according to the aesthetic conventions of those who use them are known as motifs. They are not always culturally specific; most contain lines, shapes, and other visual details that can be simplified or made more complex. Use of motifs indicates a form of shorthand; the designer can modify or expand a motif to offer a visual idea. In jewelry, motifs take on an ornamental function or are used as repetitive patterning. Many motifs, when used over and over again, turn into conventionalized designs.

Design motifs fall into two categories: representational or abstract images. Southwestern Indian smiths began working metal for adornment in the historical period when European and European American designers were preoccupied with organic and abstract decorative imagery. Indian jewelry-makers weren't interested in depicting their personal spiritual beliefs in outright representational imagery: they'd already learned to take their religion underground and replace it with referential symbols such as the dragonfly or morning star. The sacred was better represented through abstract elements such as prayer feathers, rain, wind, mountains, or in the use of natural materials such as jet, shell, or turquoise. Any depiction of a sacred spirit, like the *Yei* who aid the Navajo, needed to be carefully rendered in a form of visual shorthand.

Cuff with prayer plumes design by Michael Kabotie, c. 2004. Courtesy of Ingrid Levine.

Bracelet with butterfly motif by Raymond Sequatewa, post-1980. Courtesy of Martha Hopkins Struever.

Cuff marked with fine stamp and repoussé work, and cow head design, 1910. Courtesy of Philip Bacon Collection.

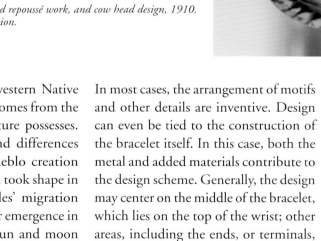

Much of the Southwestern Native designer's initial cosmos comes from the creation stories each culture possesses. There are similarities and differences between Navajo and Pueblo creation stories. The natural world took shape in the process of the peoples' migration between worlds until their emergence in the current world. The sun and moon are the responsibilities of sacred figures, and they in turn possess helpers and other beings, many of them the first animals, who populate the changing worlds. The associations of shell with water, silver with the moon, and other relationships can guide the designer.

The organization or structure of formal elements on the bracelet's surface springs from the creator's imagination.

In most cases, the arrangement of motifs and other details are inventive. Design can even be tied to the construction of the bracelet itself. In this case, both the metal and added materials contribute to the design scheme. Generally, the design may center on the middle of the bracelet, which lies on the top of the wrist; other areas, including the ends, or terminals, can carry design embellishment as well.

What are the most likely sources for design? In *Southwestern Indian Rings*, we discovered that a jeweler could draw upon three significant areas for design inspiration: craft, culture, and individualistic nature. In terms of craft, precedents and physical examples exist to guide design-making. The creator's culture provides imagery drawn from the natural, spiri-

tual, and everyday world. Equally important is the influence of popular culture. The jeweler's individual "vision" of the world determines how a design can be invented, altered, or conjoined. Personal identity is another factor related to design choice. Potential buyers find themselves mentally and visually alerted by small cues or clues; even an avant-garde work by a contemporary Native fine art jeweler will contain some sense of the maker's heritage or "Indianness."

There can be similarities in the cultural worldviews of the Navajo, Pueblo, and other Native peoples of the American Southwest. One thing all cultures held in common was the natural world around them and its distinctive features: mesas; canyons; sacred mountains; rivers; rich

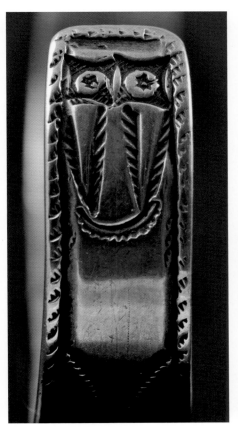

Owl image fashioned from three separate stamps instead of later single stamp, 1900. Courtesy of Philip Bacon Collection.

Large silver cuff, hammered and cold chiseled, and set with Cerrillos natural turquoise, Pueblo-made, 1910s-1920. Courtesy of Laura Anderson.

brown, red, and white vegetation; desert cacti; and wide encircling sky. As the first smiths created their crude punches and dies, they shaped stamps that would represent elements of earth and sky. Next would come representations of the elements humans live and die by: sun, moon, stars, water, wind, rain, and corn. From the water and ground came other materials, all invested in power from stories and legends: shell, coral, turquoise, and jet, plus stones for grinding corn or to hold in heat during healing ceremonies. Even colors and numbers possessed spiritual meaning.

What could be more beautiful or relevant to wear as adornment than these representations rendered as motifs? Such

design elements would carry some of the energy or life force of these objects. Add animals with clan associations or sacred spirits with specific functions to aid the people, and designs take on the power attributed to such representations.

It was an easy step from there for design motifs to be associated with symbols, something the curio dealers promoted to non-Indian buyers. Punches, dies, and stamps had been used to create varied aspects of the natural world; the shapes that were formed now served as a visual glossary for additions to adornment. These first tools made straight lines, hemispheres, and circles, all of which could be combined into such shapes as enclosures,

fences, lightning, zigzag mountain ranges, sky, and horizon. Early stamps depicted insects and butterflies, and then branched out into simple outlines of birds and animals.

Pueblo dances and rituals provided a wide variety of popular motifs for design. Pueblo "cross" symbols can be associated with star signs, war signs, and (at certain pueblos) domestic animals (Parsons, 2, 1113). Crosses can also represent directions; one curio "meaning" is of paths crossing. Enclosed crosses can be found on Ancestral Puebloan pottery and among petroglyphs. Pueblo adoption of Catholic ritual affected the use of clown and kachina masks (Parsons, 1073). Even the dragonfly has proved to be a

Hopi cuff with badger paw overlay design by Jacob Poleviyouma, 1970s. Courtesy of Robert Bauver.

Two bracelets depict Koshare and Mudhead figures by Augustine and Rosalie Pinto, Zuni Pueblo, early 1970s. Courtesy of Erik Van Itallie.

Bracelet with organic Hopi themes by Gary and Elsie Yoyokie, c. 2000. Private Collection.

Pictorial bracelet with sun, originally made for Elsie, but sold to owner's father, 1990s, Gary and Elsie Yoyokie, 1990s. Courtesy of Funny Company.

Silver bracelet with Apache dancers by Clarence Lee, c. 1992. Photograph by Danny Luwe. Courtesy of Allan and Joyce Niederman Collection.

fitting design subject: dragonfly cross necklaces made by various Pueblos' smiths looked like tribute to the Catholic religion, but actually permitted Native wearers to pay tribute to the sun god (Bird, 17).

Pueblos' various clan systems had animal and bird preferences for design. Some animals chosen for motifs include antelope or deer, badgers, bears, buffalo, snakes, and turtles. The water serpent (or *Kolowisi*) represents Pueblo reverence, and appears also as an Avanyu design. Interestingly, the parrot—a bird from ancestral days—features as an early motif. Pueblo regard for birds is another feature of early and classic silver design, and has been much revived by those artists who like old-style themes. Eagles are popular images, along with the oddly ambiguous owl. When smiths depict heartlines, they are utilizing the spirit paths seen on

traditional pottery, sand paintings, weaving, and fetish carving.

The Pueblo peoples have also contributed a number of critical designs that appear throughout the history of silver jewelry creation: prayer sticks; corn on stalks and cobs; cactus; and feathers. Designs derived from baskets, masks, and

shields emerge more confidently as tools improved in the mid-twentieth century.

Navajo and Apache jewelry-makers share an affinity for depicting natural phenomena like clouds, lightning, moon, and sun. These images, drawn from their appearance in the Southwestern sky, are motifs that appeal to all those who live

Hopi-made silver eagle design on an expansion band, c. 1990. Photograph by Danny Lewes. Courtesy of Allan and Joyce Niederman Collection.

Bird design bracelet, probably Pueblo-made, 1950s–1960s. Courtesy of Vicki Turbeville.

or travel through the landscape with its vast overhead dome of sky. Inevitably, recreations of sacred natural landmarks became food for design. From Monument Valley to Shiprock, tangible locations become part of the designer's story.

Native jewelry-makers did not take to real storytelling until they were more comfortable in fashioning figural designs. When the storyteller bracelet finally appeared, it suited both connoisseur and casual tastes; compositions generally were rectangular to fit along the bracelet's central plate. In many respects they resemble narrative vignettes from pictorial rugs.

One animal rarely found on a Native-made bracelet or any other form of jewelry is the coyote. He is known as a trickster in Native origin stories, but also serves as a symbol of witchcraft, a trait some other animals and birds share. Skinwalkers are often believed to be witches wearing coyote-skins. The stereotyped motif of the howling coyote seen in Southwestern tourist ware is decidedly non-Native in origin.

Designs for jewelry were also deeply influenced by Navajo and Pueblo weaving.

Ketoh with Yei figure design in silver and turquoise, 1940s. Courtesy of Vicki Turbeville.

A range of Zuni sun face designs on bracelets, 1950s–1970s. Courtesy of Vicki Turbeville.

Almost every silversmith had a mother, wife, or daughter who wove textiles. Whether their mother was Navajo and made saddle blankets or larger compositions for sale to the Indian trader, or a Pueblo woman weaving mantas and creating rich embroidery, smiths became consciously drawn to the harmony expressed in woven designs. The plumped-out butterfly shape found on a *ketoh* or sandcast cuff might have originated from saddle blankets. The elongated and rectilinear X-shapes on a bow guard can be seen in certain weaving compositions. Bracelets possessing contrasts between raised silver and oxidized recesses may have developed from the alternation of geometric and bold patterns in regional weaving designs. From related traditions, Pueblo mantas and *tablita* headdresses served as inspiration for silver bracelet border designs.

A possible indication of Navajo perspective on silver and stone hard goods appears in several lines from the Night Way ceremonial chant. This nine-day ceremony features the *Yei*, and is used for specific diseases that affect the head, including blindness, deafness, and insanity. During the fourth night of the ritual, the medicine man awakes the sacred masks with song and a personal prayer. Part of this chant says:

In beauty may I walk.
Goods may I acquire.
Precious stones may I acquire.
Horses may I acquire.
Sheep may I acquire…
(Matthews, 1902, 111–112)

Adornment therefore ranks as important as any of the other essential hard goods needed for a balanced life. Non-Natives intrigued by the Navajo worldview often pounce on the concept of *hózhó* in which Native appreciation of beauty was something intertwined with harmony, whereby nature and human experience sought the right measure of

33

Silver cuff with Hopi mask head design by Victor Coochytewa, late 1970s. Courtesy of Funny Company.

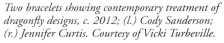

Two bracelets showing contemporary treatment of dragonfly designs, c. 2012; (l.) Cody Sanderson; (r.) Jennifer Curtis. Courtesy of Vicki Turbeville.

Knifewing bracelet inlay attributed to John Gordon Leak, and Rainbow Man bracelet inlay attributed to David Tsikewa; both have a tomahawk hallmark indicating silverwork by another smith, 1920s–1930s. Courtesy of Laura Anderson.

balance. Life lived in harmony—*hózhó*—offers an attractive, if somewhat simplified, definition of Southwestern Indian aesthetics. If we take the usual definition of aesthetics as being the philosophy of beauty, art, and taste as it applies to the individual, then we appreciate how appealing Native-made bracelets have proven to be. This Native view also meshes beautifully with our contemporary admiration for diversity.

One last point to be made is that these design choices reflect the things Native jewelry-makers deeply esteemed in the world around them. The curio trade would claim similar decorative motifs as "Indian Symbols" and make contrived explanations for what such motifs "meant." Once again, the conflict between commercialization and artistic expression resulted in confusion and tentative compromise, with those who

cared about Indian art baffled by the need to trivialize Native vision. The late twentieth-century public approval of fine craftwork and wearable art left bogus Indian designs behind, and consigned them to the low-end tourist trade.

When discussing bracelet **styles**, there remains some confusion over their designation. A good example is the identification of tribal designs with styles, as in Hopi overlay style. Overlay is a

Two green stone snake design bracelets, early twentieth century. Courtesy of Philip Bacon Collection.

"Grandmother" overlay silver bracelet with coral head by Norbert Peshlakai, post-1980. Courtesy of Martha Hopkins Struever.

technique that has been singularly associated with the noteworthy Hopi adoption of overlay in the 1930s and 1940s and its use by the Hopi Silvercraft Guild. Yet overlay was a technique used by Santo Domingo jewelers in the 1930s, and its potential would be exploited by Navajo smiths as well.

In many cases, Zuni artists have been praised so much for their lapidary work that their silver-working abilities have been glossed over. Much of this came from traders and from writers on Indian jewelry who used generalizations as explanations to consumers and readers. Yet with an artist of the stature of Horace Iule teaching metalsmithing at the Zuni Day School in the 1920s, the truth is

that more silverwork came from Zuni forges than has previously been credited.

One source of misperceptions about tribal styles derives from the pages of the 1976 collector classic publication *Skystone and Silver*. The authors interviewed popular Native smiths and jewelers. Master silversmith and longtime jewelry instructor Kenneth Begay ended his interview with the statement that "Navajos should make jewelry like the Navajos and Zunis like the Zunis…" (Rosnek, 117). Yet, later in the same book, Dr. Patrick Houlihan claims that "contemporary Indian jewelry has transcended tribal styles…" (Rosnek, 144). For more discussion on the mixed signals of the 1970s in relation to Native jewelry-making, see Chapter 6.

Similarly, confusion arises over the term "tourist style," which has been replaced by "Fred Harvey style." Technically, it would be better to refer to "Fred Harvey era jewelry design," since it signifies a period when travel and tourism greatly impacted curio or tourist work. Like rings, Southwestern Indian bracelets made excellent souvenirs of a journey to the region. In this case, "style" actually means items that show the influence of commercialization, that is, lightweight, stereotypically stylized decoration.

In addition, it should be pointed out that jewelers, like other decorative artists, can also make stylized designs. What does it mean when we say a bracelet is

Navajo sandcast cuff displays star and lightning design, c. 1960. Courtesy of Eason Eige Collection, Albuquerque, New Mexico.

Katsina mask bracelet by Charles Loloma, with ironwood, ivory, turquoise on silver, c. 1980–1982. Courtesy of Faust Gallery.

Detail of multi-stone bracelet with a Valentine heart on end; hearts were a popular motif in 1930s. Courtesy of Philip Bacon Collection.

stylized? The term refers to a certain enlargement of pattern, design, or stylistic features that appear more overt than subtle. The effect may be intentional or unconscious, depending on the maker; a piece that is stylized invariably draws attention to the forceful ordering of its visual details.

The term "style" itself has been so widely defined and applied in our society that it doesn't hurt to return to its original core meaning. A "style" is something that is done in a particular manner related to a period, person, place, or movement. When we talk about styles of decorative art, as in the case of Southwestern Indian-made jewelry, it becomes more plausible that style can refer to: a specific time (such as the term old-style), a master designer (e.g. in the style of Loloma), a specific tribe (such as Hopi style), or a general *zeitgeist* (like Native Style).

Once we take this definition into account, we can see why makers, purveyors, and consumers use "style" as much as they do. Yet such labels carry connotations, and the application of categories such as old-style, classic style, and traditional style need to be accepted in the broadest terms possible.

Detail, head of serpent.

Early overlay bracelet with abstract Avanyu design by Dean Siwingyumptewa, Hopi, c. 1948–1950. Courtesy of Karen Sires.

Wide silver cuff with swastika stamp design by Morris Robinson, Hopi, 1920s–1930s. Courtesy of Karen Sires.

Silver and multi-stone inlay hawk Zuni design, maker unknown, c. 1940. Photograph by Danny Luwe. Courtesy of Allan and Joyce Niederman Collection.

Those who become involved in the ethnic art market should be as alert to the correct usage of "style" as they have learned to be about the terms "pawn" and "reproduction." In the future, collectors need to be sensitive to the labels that Native artists apply to their creations. After years of having non-Natives speak for them, or providing design information that they think

Four stone cuffs showing emerging styles; clockwise from left: row, channel inlay, needlepoint, and cluster. Courtesy of Vicki Turbeville.

Round-wire cuff with raised stones in abstract bear paw design; may have been made by a young artist, 1930s–1940s. Courtesy of Steve and Mary Delzio, The Mexican Shack.

their customers want, today's Indian jewelers will prove to be as self-analytical as other artists in the global marketplace.

Native Style is referred to in Chapter 7. This term has arisen from Native artists directly and continues to be loosely defined. One of the most interesting principles that has arisen from this new "style" is the understanding that Native

Silver cuff with horses and mounted horse carving by Clarence Lee, c. 1980s–1990s. Courtesy of Faust Gallery.

jewelers mentally link design and fashion. Native Style is very much about contemporary, twenty-first century attitude shaped by popular culture. From skateboards to radically redesigned squash blossoms, today's Native artists let us know that they are artists first, proud to have their rich cultural heritage at hand, but very much individuals driving their aesthetic vision. In the future, design will be described on *their* terms.

A large Zuni Knifewing design cuff made in a stylized fashion, 1970s. Courtesy of Vicki Turbeville.

CHAPTER TWO

HISTORIC BRACELETS: NINETEENTH CENTURY

One indigenous form of wrist adornment made for a practical purpose was the bow guard: a leather wristlet with a metal plate added. Meant as wrist protection for those using a bow, these guards have been frequently referred to by their Navajo name *ketoh*. They are interesting to compare with early Native-made cuffs, and many examples exist of metal designs on the rectangular plate. While *ketohs* were primarily for men's use, the decorative motifs are strong but not distinctively masculine. The resultant designs are rectilinear forms made from early metal incising tools; both *ketohs* and early cuff bracelets share aesthetic affinities. For example, nineteenth-century smiths made symmetrical lines that curved, crossed, or bisected the surface space.

Ketohs continued to be made well after bow-and-arrow hunting had diminished. They regularly featured in sacred and social dances. Early designs resemble cast work and are curved when the smith hammers the plate over a bracelet mandrel (Branson I, 40). The metal plate lent itself to design experimentation, and smiths attempted to make patterns that brought out parallel lines, stamps that created shadows and contrasts on the metal surface, and the addition of small stones in a central location. By the time *ketohs* became part of ceremonial dress only, improved silver and tools rendered the results more sophisticated in effect.

Metalworking came to the Southwest first with Mexican leatherworkers, and then with the arrival of the U.S. Army, freed up after the Civil War to pursue potential opponents of American westward expansion. The transmission of metalworking for Navajo and Pueblo use was spurred by social developments. In the case of the Navajo, these developments were initially traumatic in nature.

Historian Hampton Sides wrote about Navajo spirit in his epic *Blood and Thunder*, in which he describes Kit Carson's rout of the tribe in the 1860s. In the book, Sides speaks of the Navajo as being the "...strongest, richest, and most creatively adaptable of all the raiding tribes" (Sides, 17). Creativity, of course, is not exclusive to any one activity, like raiding, or any one group. Yet this description of the Navajo as being creatively

adaptable proves true again and again, particularly when it came to working metal. Even as other tribes in the Southwest gained access to instruction in metalsmithing, Navajo ingenuity stands out. While the Navajo people had been acquainted with metalworking prior to their Long Walk (including historical reports that describe them trading and wearing Mexican silver ornaments as early as 1821), they took ownership of the process in a remarkably short amount of time (Frank, 4). Informer reports have Navajo smiths spreading the craft not long after their return to *Dinetah*.

Navajo industriousness is what strikes us when we reflect on how they rebounded after their devastating internment at Fort Sumner, New Mexico (1864-68). Throughout the 1870s and 1880s, the U.S. Army continued clearing the West of defiant Indian tribes and bands. Consider the state of the Sioux after their defeat and massacre at Wounded Knee in 1890; Army payback for their earlier victory over Lieutenant Colonel George Armstrong Custer kept the survivors hungry, subdued, and dependent on military agencies. During the 1880s, the Army pursued Apache renegades Geronimo and Cochise through Arizona before they were vanquished. In contrast, by this time Navajos had already begun the process of working iron, copper, brass, and a metal they soon vastly preferred—silver.

The settled Pueblo Indians—who were never relocated or interned—had closer contact with Mexican settlers and the incoming European Americans traversing the Santa Fe Trail. The proximity of Rio Grande Pueblos to the territory of New Mexico's two largest towns, Albuquerque and Santa Fe, gave Native men employment possibilities as the curio trade began in earnest in the 1890s.

The Navajo, still hard at work repairing their tribal fortunes, looked around for opportunities. Recorded accounts have them expert in blacksmithing skills, with a growing network of craft transmission. Native smiths started with bridle bits, harness and wagon wheel repairs, and made small metal objects (such as canteens and tweezers) for local Army men. They were adept at repurposing copper wire, iron scraps, and building simple forges from smooth rocks and makeshift iron anvils. Navajo smiths were reported by informants to have transmitted silver craft to the Hopi and the western pueblo of Zuni near the end of the nineteenth century.

Navajo smiths redoubled their efforts when non-Native traders set up shop on the Navajo reservation and in border towns. These traders began importing materials to aid silverwork and took Indian-made pieces as collateral for store credit. At the same time, Pueblo smiths found non-Native townspeople who favored their metalwork, along with a small but steady trickle of tourists.

An examination of bracelets made between 1868 and 1900 reveals the types of wrist adornment that Native smiths pursued when starting their craft. A large amount of this work has been lost over the decades: melted down, altered, or buried with the original owners. Fine examples that have survived—those now collected in museums and the ones that are obtainable through the antique Indian art market—are valued not just for their workmanship but also for their historic rarity. We can understand their designs better when we look at them with the analytical eye of the experts who coined the phrase "First Phase"; recognize influences from other cultures; and sort decorative motifs from solid silver, stone set, and cast bracelets.

First Phase

The transmission of the craft is well recorded in John Adair's *The Navajo and Pueblo Silversmiths* of 1944, based on research conducted around 1938. In terms of design history, pieces created before 1900 reflect the most significant

wants of their makers. Virtually every bracelet made at this time was a bangle or wider cuff. There was little to distinguish between a bracelet made for a man, woman, or child except its circumference. The earliest construction techniques available in 1868 were silver forged from cast ingots, chisel cutting, and hand-drawn and forged wire. Forge soldering and openwork casting, using a direct design, followed within the next ten years or so. Most bracelets produced during this time were remarkable for being handsome despite the rudimentary tools employed for their creation.

The first bracelets were formed from three specific types of cuffs. The first category was composed of thin bangles

with a triangular cross-section; this type corresponded closely to those bangles worn earlier in the century by Plains Indians. The second bracelet type consisted of a flat, broad band that had been annealed and hammered into shape. The third category of form was created from two (sometimes three) pieces of heavy round silver wire twisted together. During the First Phase decades, these three types were combined for a more sophisticated sculptural effect.

New tools and techniques marked the end of the First Phase and the close of the nineteenth century. Techniques like hand-drawn and forged wire, and heavy overlapping bezels, were replaced by machine-processed silver wire in a variety of gauges, blowtorch soldering,

Silver Mexican bracelet made at Taxco studio, mid-twentieth century; works from this city's studios influenced Southwestern Native design. Courtesy of Territorial Indian Arts.

Three ingot silver flat cuffs with stamp work and repoussé, 1890s–1910s. Courtesy of Ken Wolf.

thin bezel settings, and improved stamps for decoration. As with most time periods, however, 1900 didn't represent an absolute end to First Phase techniques: some smiths, especially those living in isolated locations, acquired these newer processes later, and continued using old awls, chisels, and dies well into the new century.

In fact, it's critical at this point to note that the oldest techniques would never really go away. They were revived in the years ahead as yet another tribute to the creativity of the first Native smiths. The effects achieved by early tools were pleasing, and they added a historical dimension to the craft. Some contemporary Native jewelers, such as Ron Bedonie, still use cold chisel cutting as a means of detailing surface decoration.

Close-up of "serape" stamp design on bracelet. Courtesy of Ken Wolf.

Group of eight very early silver bracelets, including a single thin bangle, two wide swedged cuffs, and an early example of repoussé, late 1800s to early 1900s. Courtesy of Philip Bacon Collection.

Early Hopi silver bracelet showing Mexican influence and primitive plate, c. 1905. Courtesy of Eason Eige Collection, Albuquerque, NM.

The earliest First Phase decoration is notably rectilinear since the main tools for creating patterns and designs—labor-intensive devices such as scratch and rocker-engraving, cold chisel stamping, and rough awls and files—all made straight lines. With some effort, punches could be used to make circles. As a result, early surface patterning on bracelets tends to be simple, well-proportioned, and understated. Once stamps became more prevalent, designs achieved more curvilinear and complex patterning. The real fine-tuning of bracelet design took place after 1900, aided by repoussé and machine-cut stones.

Once a bracelet's basic construction was established, the smith began considering how its design could be enhanced. Where did the design impulses of the indigenous smiths of the American Southwest come from? The Native smith's aesthetic sensibilities were undoubtedly shaped by harmony, balance, nature, and an innate appreciation for symmetry. Nonetheless, some amount of outside influence informs First Phase designs.

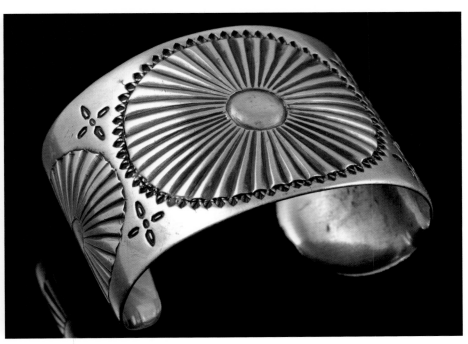

Three bracelets showing transition of bangles into bands, 1880s. Courtesy of Philip Bacon Collection.

Navajo cuff with sunburst design from simple handmade stamps, c. 1885–90. Courtesy of Karen Sires.

Silver bracelet with design from a single handmade stamp, 1890. Courtesy of Karen Sires.

Outside Influences

Three categories of outside cultural influences had an impact on the earliest Southwestern Native jewelry and bracelet production:

a. Eastern and northern Plains indigenous jewelry attracted Navajo and Pueblo attention, usually through social contact at events like the annual fall trade fair at Taos Pueblo.

b. Mexican and Spanish jewelry worn by Hispanic settlers affected early design.

c. Some forms of adornment brought west by European American settlers could be seen and noticed by the early smiths.

When we consider the combination of culture, craft, and individualistic expression, it makes sense that the cuff shape preferred by other Native tribes would also become the form of choice for Southwestern Native smiths.

The Plains tribes had been wearing metal ornaments for most of the nineteenth century. Fur traders venturing past the Mississippi River brought Eastern Native silverwork. Bracelets tended to be larger-scale and worn as armlets above the elbow. Many of these armlets had delicately chased designs, yet those Navajo and Pueblo who acquired ornaments through trade with other tribes showed a clear preference for Plains narrow bangles over the bigger cuff shapes; still, these items were not forgotten once Southwestern Native metalsmithing began in earnest.

Nineteenth-century Mexican jewelry took its design from Spanish and Roman Catholic sources. Its greatest influence may lie in the skillful use of wire filigree adopted by Navajo and Pueblo smiths; even this embellishment required several decades of perfecting and the use of better materials and tools. The visual attractiveness of wire seen in Mexican adornment was well noted by the early Native smiths of the Southwest.

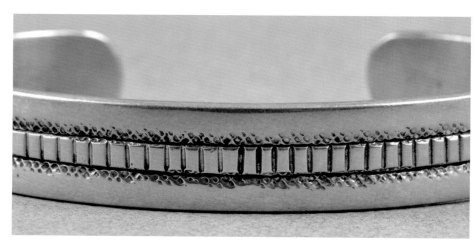

Silver cuff with designs incised in cold chisel, no hallmark, early twentieth century. Courtesy of Norman L. Sandfield.

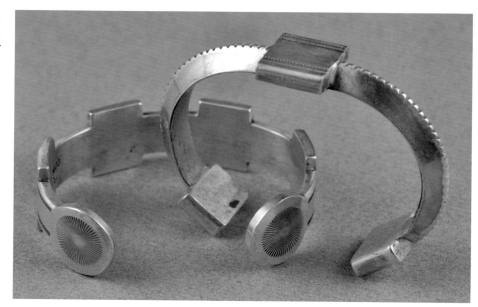

A revival of what two early Pueblo bangles would look like, by Mike Bird-Romero, 1980s. Courtesy of Martha Hopkins Struever.

Another direct inspiration would come from the silver workshops of Taxco, which influenced 1920s and later designs.

European American jewelry worn by those who lived in the Southwest poses a greater question of influence. Bracelets of this background tended to be for women and were usually hinged or otherwise fastened. Pre-Civil War era bracelets were generally made from gold, and cabochon garnet settings were popular. Children's bracelets were devised with adjustable closures. Cuffs do appear around the 1860s, particularly for pieces that were enameled, and some were created with *petra dura* or gutta-percha center plaques. Slim bangles, in rolled silver, yellow gold, and gold over brass, appeared in the 1880s

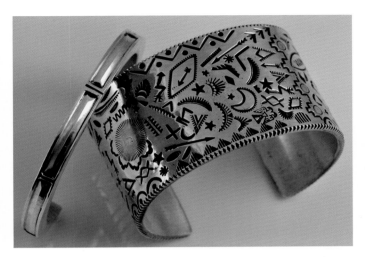

Old-style Pueblo silver bangle, and silver cuff marked with a variety of stamps by Mike Bird-Romero, 2010. Courtesy of Eason Eige Collection, Albuquerque, NM.

Silver cuff with gold buffaloes overlay, by Paul Szabo, Sioux. 1990s. Courtesy of Allan and Joyce Niederman Collection.

and 1890s. Persian turquoise and jet materials show up during this time as well. Cuffs with hinges are plentiful by 1900. Some decorative motifs popular for American bracelets in the mid- to later nineteenth century were the sinuous snake and the dragonfly. Nevertheless, Native smiths adhered to the cuff form while dropping such options as hinges and adjustable fasteners; experiments with link bracelets (going back as early as 1920) and circular bangles ensued in the early to mid-twentieth century, but, on the whole, Native taste for the cuff prevailed.

Solid Metal Bracelets

The majority of solid metal bracelets made during the First Phase were those that required hammering and annealing. A smaller percentage of solid bracelets would be cast in a mold from coin silver: these will be discussed later on. Southwestern Natives did acquire German silver Plains bangles with simple incised lines, and this style was reproduced in both copper and silver. While some smiths use German silver to this day, it always seems to have been a minority choice. Native smiths of the Southwest instead turned to silver from coins—U.S. or Mexican—melted into ingots. The U.S. government banned the use of currency as ingot silver around 1890, but this didn't stop the flow immediately.

First Phase smiths worked with very crude forges and tools. What they wrought, however, was remarkable in terms of design purity and aesthetic merit. Generally, they worked brass and copper into adornment, before taking on silver. Many contemporary Native jewelers today also start out with these metals. The switch to silver, however, was overwhelming after 1880. Solid silver bracelets were the easiest to make, even with primitive resources. Once the silver had been melted into cast ingots, it could be heated, shaped on a round forge, hammered into flatness and then wrought into cuff shape, with an opening left for adjustment.

The bracelet would be bent into shape, with a flat band (or center plate) at the top of the wrist that would extend in a curve to the terminals on each end of the cuff. All this surface space was capable of holding decoration, but the center plate usually served as the main focus for the design. Early First Phase smiths created a rhythmic repetition across the entire curved band. Roughly around 1900, the number of compound, composite solid metal bracelets greatly increased. Two favorite modes of elaboration involved building the band's width through ridging or carination, or by adding twisted wire.

Curvilinear designs were introduced with the addition of more vivid stamps and repoussé. By 1900, specific stamps for arrows and swastikas were routinely used. Variations on the arrow can be found in stamps that range from crescents to butterflies. (The swastika piqued Anglos' interest since it could be found in ancient Europe, but the Native version was based on whirling logs.) Stamps with curved forms depicted new types of motifs while repoussé altered the surface of the flat band.

The first writers on early Indian jewelry prized plain silver bracelets. Over

Silver cuff with peyote bird by Bruce Caesar, a design much loved by his father, noted Pawnee silversmith Julius Caesar, 1970s–1980s. Courtesy of Allan and Joyce Niederman Collection.

Native Northwest Coast silver band with early design and hinged back, c. 1900. Courtesy of Doug and Kris Sill Collection.

and over again, H.P. Mera and other experts extolled the aesthetic effect of the metal cuff and how its Native maker chose to create effective patterning. These authorities became alarmed by the growing trend toward ornamenting bracelets. The replacement of stamped motifs with stonework upset their appreciation of early designs. Mera and others most liked to track seemingly enduring design elements or motifs, either geometric or organic in nature, achieved by a judicious combination of stamping, incising, and punch work, and rendered texturally interesting through repoussé.

Stone Set Bracelets

There is some disagreement about when Natives adopted stone setting on bracelets. Most historians agree that stone setting began in the 1880s, while others claim that this craft work really came into being in the 1890s. The setting of single stones most likely dates to the

Late nineteenth-century cuff, hammered from coins with drilled bead stone and evidence of early embossing. Courtesy of Steve and Mary Delzio, The Mexican Shack.

Two historic bracelets each set with a single stone, 1890s. Courtesy of Ken Wolf.

Two single green stone bracelets, 1890s–1910s. Courtesy of Philip Bacon Collection.

Three coin and ingot silver Pueblo cuffs display strong organic stamping, c. 1890s–1910. Courtesy of Laura Anderson.

Two bracelets with repoussé, done by the same artist (note the identical stamping around the repoussé), 1890s. Courtesy of Philip Bacon Collection.

Six cuffs accented with differing silver studs or raindrop beads, 1890s to 1920s. Courtesy of Philip Bacon Collection.

Verso and terminals of a cuff from the late 1800s. Courtesy of Philip Bacon Collection.

1880s. Multiple stone setting can be traced to the last decade of the century with more certainty. The more facile and sophisticated combination of stone and silver characterizes the core concept of a Southwestern Indian bracelet, despite the enduring classicism of solid silver bracelets minus settings.

The Pueblo people already had a tradition of wearing adornment from natural materials. Early bracelets were carved from bone, jet, and wood. Local materials were strung into necklaces, ranging from shell obtained from trade to garnets and turquoise. Natives hand mined green turquoise for centuries from several locations near present-day Cerrillos, New Mexico. Combining stone and metal was a natural impulse, but how could these materials adhere to each other? Some early pieces show stones crudely soldered to a metal plate, but a holding rim of metal, known as a bezel, was soon fashioned. The first bezels were makeshift affairs. Some only ran halfway up the side of a stone.

Did the number of stones set in a cuff have any significance? Native peoples did have an affinity for certain groups of numbers. It's interesting to speculate, after looking at many examples of early stone and silver bracelets that odd numbers predominate: one, three, five, and seven stones set around a band. When one talks to contemporary silversmiths, however, they are apt to mention four and six as

These thin triangular carinated bangles with set stones show the transformation from a flat band into sculptural pieces, 1890s–1920s. Courtesy of Philip Bacon Collection.

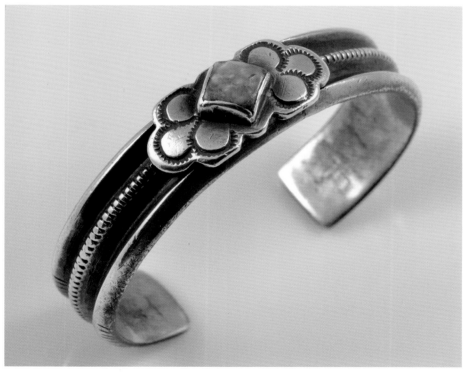

Example of early appliqué and use of chisels, 1890s. Courtesy of Philip Bacon Collection.

preferred numbers, in reference to the four or six directions.

The First Phase development of bezels, or mounts, for stones can be traced through observation of the gradual precision that went into their making. Handmade bezels eventually reached the top of a stone and made a narrow frame for the setting. Serrated bezels started appearing with more frequency in the 1890s. Post-1900 bezels attained a greater precision as Native smiths took advantage of the technical means to better make thin bezel sets.

Turquoise was clearly the stone of choice for Navajo and Pueblo smiths. This material wasn't plentiful in the nineteenth century, however, so many early designs featured one or two stones as central decoration on bracelets. Multitudes of stones didn't become viable until the period between 1900 and

Early bracelet with square-cut green stone and cold chisel work, 1880s–1890s. Courtesy of Vicki Turbeville.

Side view of terminals.

Six single-stone cuffs set with some unusually cut stones, showing historic era progression of increased decoration, late nineteenth century to 1920s. Courtesy of Philip Bacon Collection.

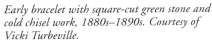

Black box of silver and stone bracelets. Courtesy of Philip Bacon Collection.

1930. Indian traders like Lorenzo Hubbell played a large role in obtaining hand-cut and polished stones; these middlemen were known to send local material out to the East Coast and even Europe. During the First Phase and early 1900s, Hubbell and others imported substitute materials like glass beads and cabochons. A number of pre-1900 bracelets can be found that have been set with a repurposed drilled bead. Bedinger points out that the 1920s brought increased turquoise to the reservation, and "stones all around" bracelets grew in number,

accompanied by well-made bezels and applique decoration—often raindrops (Bedinger, 95).

The lack of turquoise in this time period allowed the early experts to develop strong preferences for all-silver band bracelets. Yet, it should be stressed that this was a non-Native aesthetic choice. Indians of the Southwest cherished the spiritual properties of the stones that smiths set in bracelets, and this appreciation can still be seen in the predominance of multiple-stone-set jewelry worn by tribal dancers.

Hopi turquoise and silver bracelet with drilled bead, c. 1900. Courtesy of Eason Eige Collection. Albuquerque, NM.

Five early Navajo bracelets with good stamp work, showing saw tooth and square bezels made at this time, 1890–1910. Courtesy of Karen Sires.

Three bracelets, 1880–1900, spanning turn of the century designs. Courtesy of Michael Horsley.

Cast Bracelets

Sandcast bracelets can be readily identified as a Southwestern Indian jewelry form. They are seriously sculptural in nature. While some examples may have been earlier, 1875 most often appears in anthropological and historical accounts as the official start for sustained work in casting. From the beginning, however, Native smiths discovered that this labor-intensive process frequently resulted in failure, leaving broken pieces of mold and metal. After early experiments, volcanic tufa, a porous form of sandstone, was used for most molds.

Smiths liked the ability to create a very intricate form in just one step. Early

Two cuffs with experimental stamping: (top) ingot silver with crudely cut stone and bezel; (bottom) larger cuff of hammered silver, 1890s–1910. Private Collection.

Three ketohs (from left): filed design, 1880s; butterfly and other design from turn of the twentieth century (1890–1910). Courtesy of Michael Horsley.

Two bracelets where raindrops have been carved and cast into the mold: one cuff is by an unknown Navajo or Zuni maker, the multi-stone piece is signed by Juan Dedios, mid-twentieth century. Courtesy of Robert Bauver.

Terminals of the two bracelets.

examples demonstrate how Native smiths labored over the casting process; some bracelets were cast flat, show pitting from annealing, or were cast in two sections. Eventually, wide bands could be cast in one piece. Some pieces were cast with space for a stone. Other smiths chose to carve into the mold or used two-piece molds. Then, melted silver ingots were poured into the hollows. These carved sections produced openwork for the actual bracelet form. Decorative elements could be added. The first cast bracelets were rather heavy creations. Sometimes it proved difficult to melt the silver, and a number of pieces were made from two halves soldered together (Bedinger, 97).

Once liberated from early awkward craft endeavors, cast works were enhanced by ridging, strong stamping, and the introduction of twisted wire for decorative or structural purposes. The Navajo Guild encouraged casting based on older and plainer styles. Massive pieces weren't unknown by midcentury, but skillful openwork would always trump baroque elements. While casting has been most often associated with Navajo design impulses, including those with massive qualities, recent research has revealed that Pueblo

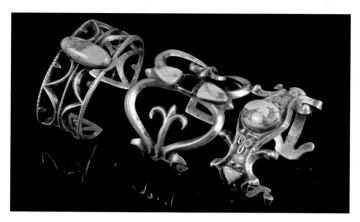

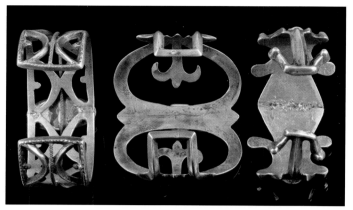

Three cast bracelets that have been constructed by joining two separate cast halves, Navajo, 1930s–1940s; such casting often had other decorative silver units applied. Courtesy of Robert Bauver.

Back of the bracelets.

Two cast bracelets by Charlie Houck, Navajo, late 1930s-1940s, an expert caster known for his delicate work with restrained stampwork. Courtesy of Robert Bauver.

smiths, especially Zuni jewelers, were also learning to make cast pieces. Some bracelets by Dan Simplicio, for example, show evidence of a casting foundation. Juan Dedios, too, worked with two-piece molds.

The tactile elements of a cast bracelet are glorious. The fact that there are irregularities in outline and mass does not overcome the sculptural elegance of such a cuff. The process of casting in

Sides of bracelets showing naja and rosette designs.

sand brought a darker surface to light, one granular in texture. Anyone who studies multiple examples of cast pieces from this early period can sense the original smiths' remarkable creative adaptability in full force. One wonders how many failed attempts occurred before the production of a single extraordinary bracelet. Those who experimented at a time when the process was slow, laborious, and ripe for failure demonstrate an unerring perseverance. The use of a local material such as tufa rock makes this handiwork proudly regional in nature.

Early twentieth-century cast piece with stamping. Courtesy of Robert Bauver.

Recent (last quarter of twentieth century/contemporary) cast cuff shows unusual highly sculptural design. Courtesy of Robert Bauver.

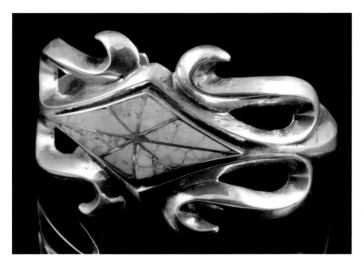

Typical midcentury Navajo cast bracelet with inlay center added, possibly Zuni, 1950s–1960s. Courtesy of Robert Bauver.

Cast bracelet with stamped ingot band and cast elements set with multiple stones, Navajo or Zuni, showing maturation of style, 1930s. Courtesy of Karen Sires.

Three cast bracelets, probably Navajo, 1940s–1960s. Courtesy of Allan and Joyce Niederman Collection.

An early twentieth-century cast bracelet. Courtesy of Karen Sires.

Commercial mass-producers of lightweight Indian jewelry turned to spin casting in 1960 in an effort to claim some of sandcasting's inherent design vitality. Cast cuffs become especially popular in the 1970s, and techniques were added to ensure a smoother finish. Bedinger's *Indian Silverwork* (1973) spoke of cast pieces as having "bold originality," pointing out how the "elaborate openwork" possessed "highly irregular outlines" (Bedinger, 33). Jewelers working after 1980 enjoyed exploring other forms of casting, cognizant of the fact that midcentury artists like Loloma had already made themselves masters of lost-wax casting.

While early cast bracelets constituted a smaller number of forged cuffs, they certainly fired both Native and non-Native imaginations. Their sculptural qualities, fine proportions, and design originality, along with the fact that they weren't easy to make and often broke their molds, heightened this attraction. In addition, the irregularities of outline and porous surface gave them a very unique appeal. Sometimes these pieces show evidence of cracking or later attempts at annealing. Collectors of early cast bracelets admire the complexity of the craft process and the resultant aesthetic beauty of these cuffs.

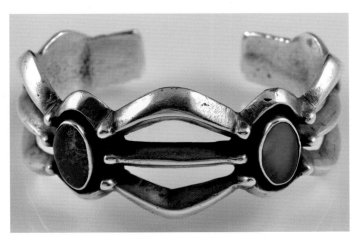

Early cast bracelet with turquoise, first quarter of twentieth century. Courtesy of Karen Sires.

This silver cast bracelet with coral stones by Mary Marie (Navajo), 1960s–1970s, shows a new treatment of an older cast style. Courtesy of Robert Bauver.

Three cast "spider" bracelets by Juan Dedios, 1930s–1940s. Courtesy of Karen Sires.

Cast bracelet set with three-stone turquoise by Horace Iule, Zuni Pueblo, mid-twentieth century. Courtesy of Karen Sires.

CHAPTER THREE

HISTORIC BRACELETS: 1900-1930

Silversmiths working prior to 1900 were already inventive, but the growing facility of metalworking in the first three decades of the new century pushed design to new highs. This was the time when culture, craft, and individualistic effort came together to produce the quintessential Indian bracelet. Such success in design achievement would soon be hailed as "classic." After 1980, those in the antique Indian arts market would also apply this label to well-made bracelets created between 1930 and 1949.

The period 1900-1930 offers us a chance to evaluate Native-made bracelets by both craft and design. Since commercialization was well established by this time, a struggle ensued over determining the purity of Native design. Plenty of non-Native influence can be recorded, from the activities of the Fred Harvey Company's Indian Department to the efforts of non-Native patrons of the Santa Fe Indian Market and non-Native Indian trader dealers at the Gallup Inter-Tribal Ceremonial.

Improved metalcraft materials and tools introduced in this period directly impacted construction and design. For example, when saws and hacksaws became available after 1900, they quickly replaced the cold chisel and its limitation of making only straight-line patterning. Sterling silver, along with machine-processed silver sheets and wire, was easier to work than coin silver. Commercial solder used with a blowtorch made such constructions as bezel housing much easier. Even sandpaper made the process of metalworking less fatiguing. Hence, the smith had more opportunity for conceiving designs.

The creativity that resulted made bracelets especially desirable. If we look for trends and tendencies, a number of

Four row bracelets, made with heavy-gauge twisted wire and heavy silver terminal caps, set with natural turquoise, 1900s–1910s. Courtesy of Laura Anderson.

Four bracelets with interesting terminals, 1900–1930s. Courtesy of Laura Anderson.

A ketoh with parrot and whirling logs, 1920s. Courtesy of Paul and Valerie Piazza.

innovations emerge. Silversmiths working after 1900 made pieces that built upon the original trio of triangular band, flat band, and twisted wire cuff forms. Carinated, or keeled, bracelets appeared in the 1920s, accentuated by better filing or ridging. Sandcast pieces might have ridged elements or twisted wire added to build up the cuff's width. Even filing began to approximate the look of twisted wire. Elongated repoussé appears in the 1900s, sometimes offsetting sinuous snake designs. By the 1920s and 1930s, bracelets featured unusually shaped stones in teardrop and diamond shapes. "Raindrops"—soldered studs of rounded silver that punctuate a bracelet's surface decoration—served as tactile statements by the 1920s.

Geometric designs remained predominant. Stones set on bracelets ranged from very large single stones to a profusion of stones in neat bezel frames. Less common were naturalistic images like animal shapes and petroglyph-like stamps of human figures. Also seen were motifs of hands, which can be traced back to Plains and Spanish colonial metalwork (Frank, 179). Figural designs, however, were inevitable given the tastes of non-Native consumers. Many Native silversmiths found themselves caught between the demands of religious privacy and respect and the hunger for depictions of sacred spirits and ceremonial attendants. One of the greatest tourist draws in early twentieth-century Southwestern travel was the Indian dance, whether sacred or social. There, visitors noted the large-scale jewelry pieces, including cuffs, worn by dancers on the plaza.

Through the nineteenth century, Navajo and Pueblo metal bracelets often seemed indistinguishable. By 1915, however, Santo Domingo and Zuni

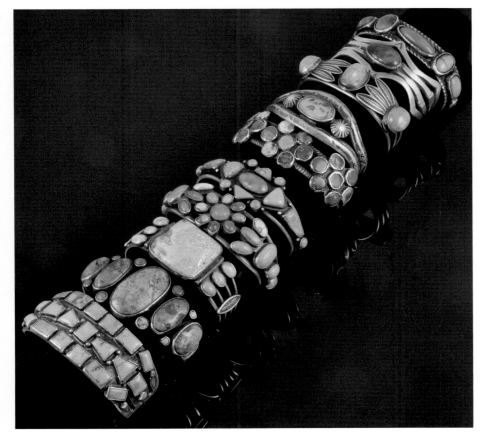

Two silver bracelets with profiles on terminals: thinner band (l.) is 1890–1900; other (r.) is from 1920. Courtesy of Karen Sires.

Three soldered bangles decorated with cold chisel, and one single-stone bangle with hands as terminals, c. 1915. Courtesy of Laura Anderson.

Ten cluster bracelets with green stones, early twentieth century. Courtesy of Laura Anderson.

jewelry began to take on a certain identity, marked by the greater use of stones than silver for decoration. Pueblo lapidaries used mosaic and crude channel inlay, and started to develop a small repertoire of figural designs. At the same time, their taste for flat-cut stone work gave rise in the 1920s to stone clusters and rows arranged on bracelets and other jewelry forms.

Between 1900 and 1930, we can see the word "style" become applied to certain types of Native-made jewelry forms. Tentative differences between Navajo and Pueblo pieces were drawn. The first non-Native chroniclers of jewelry history claimed that 1900 to 1930 should be considered a "transitional period" for Indian jewelry; works after this date were considered to be irredeemably tainted by the demands of commercialism. This sort of "hand wringing" increased among those writing about jewelry design in the 1930s and 1940s.

Transitional Period

This term for the period between 1900 and 1930 refers largely to the changeover from cruder tools to those producing more sophisticated effects on metal. Such a term best reflects the ethnographic judgment of non-Native chroniclers concerned with historical definitions and categorizations. "Transitional Period" is a viable anthropological term for noting major craft changes but is less effective when attempting to char-acterize the impact of social change on Native cultures. This is not to say that changes weren't occurring, but the tempo of social change and popular culture impact increased more rapidly after World War II.

Nevertheless, this thirty-year period is marked by design advances related to improved access to materials and tools. More bracelets were made with stones in settings, and the sophistication of bezels, appliqué, and embellishment grew to keep pace with demand. The arrival of commercial dies and stamps aided smiths, many of whom continued to fashion their own stamp motifs. The taste for strongly marked silver cuffs continued. Figural compositions appeared occasionally. For the earliest writers of Indian jewelry history, worry about the encroachment of the curio trade on Native design made 1930 a cut-off in terms of design "purity."

A much better designation than "transitional period" would be to bring together post-1868 to 1930 works as the time of traditional or "historic" jewelry creation. Bracelets made between 1868 and 1930 reflect a love of the craft that was guided by traditional values and world views. It would be an error, however, to claim that historic Native-made jewelry design, including bracelets, was free of commercial influence.

However, even the definition of "traditional" needs some reevaluation, since it has been casually applied in literature on Southwestern Indian arts. Generally, "traditional" is meant to indicate design that has a long history of usage, with this design remaining relatively free from outside influences. Anthropologists were particularly keen to uphold "traditional"

Silver band with symmetrical repoussé design, 1910s. Courtesy of Ken Wolf.

(l.) A rolled ingot cuff; (r.) a hammered silver bracelet with button design repoussé on end, 1920s. Courtesy of Ken Wolf.

Thick silver bracelet with stones on terminals, 1915. Courtesy of Ken Wolf.

Filed, chiseled, and stamped all-silver "flat top" bracelets, 1900–1920s. Courtesy of Philip Bacon Collection.

Cuff with three-stone commercially high-domed turquoise: one green stone, two blue. Serrated bezels may have been opened for stone replacement. Silver is filed to look like twisted wire, 1910s. Courtesy of Ken Wolf.

arts, especially in the face of the singular hardships Southwestern tribes faced in the early twentieth century, such as livestock reduction, children sent to boarding schools to strip them of their culture, and dwindling populations. When we note that the establishment of the influential Indian arts markets in Santa Fe and Gallup both occurred in the early 1920s, it makes sense that many people saw the need to link patronage with economic opportunity.

Indian metal jewelry creation was relatively new. Historic era smiths made pieces to please themselves and others, since they wanted work that gave them

Six stone set bracelets with heavy twisted wire, late 1910s to 1920s. Courtesy of Philip Bacon Collection.

Two cuffs with Pueblo-style stamping and native cut stones, 1920s. Courtesy of Philip Bacon Collection.

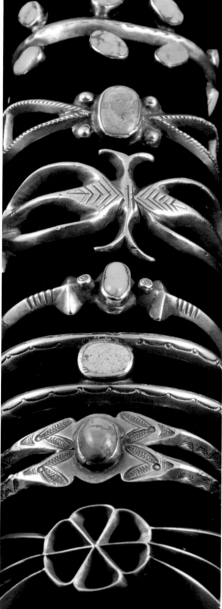

Seven cast bracelets showing a variety of styles, early twentieth century. Courtesy of Philip Bacon Collection.

money or trading-post credit. By the time John Adair did his field research in New Mexico and Arizona in the 1930s, he was able to reach first- or second-generation smiths and those who had been taught by them. In other words, Adair had access to the living memory of the first Navajo and Pueblo metalworkers.

Looking at their designs, it becomes easy to point to their works as being traditional in nature. Unfortunately, much pre-1900 silverwork was melted down or buried. Jewelry made between 1900 and 1930, including bracelets that resembled earlier styles, assumed a new authority, being better crafted in terms

of technique. No matter that traditional didn't mean works of a hundred years or more (as it does when applied to pottery and weaving), Southwestern Indian jewelry-makers had established a norm for their early designs.

Three heavy-gauge silver bracelets with interesting sides and terminals, early twentieth century. Courtesy of Philip Bacon Collection.

Geometric Designs

A general truism for the early period of Native silverwork in the Southwest has been to distinguish Navajo design as being more fully geometric, while Pueblo designs favor the organic and figural. The first smiths created abstract geometric patterns while working with simple tools such as rocker engraving and cold chisels. Tools created and available after 1900 were greatly improved in terms of their ability to make lines, curves, and other shapes.

Bracelets between 1900 and 1930 now featured stones in unusual shapes, from teardrops to rectangular, and square diamonds stood on end. These stones, however, most often appeared within a carefully delineated, geometrically shaped pattern. An early twentieth-century

Carinated bracelet with strong stamps, 1920s–1930s. Courtesy of Philip Bacon Collection.

Nine three-stone silver bracelets, late nineteenth century to 1930. Courtesy of Philip Bacon Collection.

Examples of organic floral stamps showing Mexican influence, early 1900s. Courtesy of Philip Bacon Collection.

colored postcard, produced by the Fred Harvey Company and Detroit Publishing Co., depicts a "Navaho" silversmith working on a bracelet mandrel at the Indian Building in Albuquerque. The last sentence of the short postcard description on the back reads: "The geometric forms that prevale [sic] in the designs usually have a significance."

The aesthetic tastes and preferences of someone brought up in Western civilization generally lean toward the symmetrical. Ancient Greek architecture and arts were based on rigorously symmetrical proportions. Some of the most successful design elements in

Four ketohs with cast openwork, three with stones, first half of twentieth century. Courtesy of Philip Bacon Collection.

Three Navajo cuffs with repoussé and distinctive stamps, early 1900s. Courtesy of Philip Bacon Collection.

Three silver cuffs with domed button centers, 1920–1930s. Courtesy of Philip Bacon Collection.

Ketoh with Hopi Guild mark and hallmark of Valjean Joshevema, 1940s; another with heavy sheet silver and repoussé, 1910s–1920s. Courtesy of Philip Bacon Collection.

Four butterfly cluster bracelets from the 1930s. Courtesy of Philip Bacon Collection.

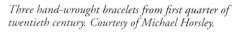

Navajo bracelet with four flush-set green stones, early 1900s. Courtesy of Philip Bacon Collection.

Three hand-wrought bracelets from first quarter of twentieth century. Courtesy of Michael Horsley.

Two Navajo bracelets with interestingly set small stones and round pulled wire; stones are divided by vertical double small stones, 1920s –1930s. Courtesy of Michael Horsley.

Three silver ingot bracelets with early deep carved filing; two are Navajo and third may be Pueblo, c. 1930. Courtesy of Joan Caballero.

Three silver ingot bracelets, one a child's bangle, from Isleta Pueblo, c. 1900–1910. Courtesy of Joan Caballero.

Silver ingot bracelet with stamp work and repoussé, set with oval turquoise stones, c. 1915–1925. Courtesy of Joan Caballero.

historic Navajo and Pueblo jewelry resemble the scroll and fret. If we look at mainstream European and American modes predominant in the first half-century of Indian silverwork, we see that neoclassic, Beaux-Arts, art nouveau, and early art deco compare well with Native-made design.

Early modernism was an aesthetic complement to historic Indian jewelry design, and nowhere was this more evident than on the bracelet. Even pre-1930 wire bracelets possessed a satisfying geometry. Some all-silver bands contain an austere linearity; later, improved tools brought unchecked curves and arabesques to break up the straight lines, but the innate symmetry inherent in the design remains.

Figural Designs

Some First Phase bracelets show designs incised or stamped with organic forms. These tend to be butterflies, insects, or snake shapes. Pueblo silversmiths showed an early inclination to make organic forms part of the overall design of an ornament. Early stamps and dies confirm a taste for patterning natural objects. However, figural designs for bracelets begin to appear in earnest between 1900 and 1930. A fine silver bracelet depicting a wolf dating back to the early 1920s can be found in a private collection (Frank, 137). Variations on the thunderbird and water serpent are also early figural motifs.

Design sources for post-1900 jewelers were most likely to come from petroglyphs and Pueblo pottery. Two creatures, the dragonfly and the snake, were already mainstream American jewelry design favorites. Those who wrote about the early jewelry claimed that snake designs were made more comfortably by Pueblo jewelers than Navajos. Nevertheless, from an early period Native smiths were making small die stamps for both creatures. Some early stamps show how closely butterfly and dragonfly forms resemble each other.

Two interesting early animal design forms were steer and deer heads, seen most often in Pueblo—especially Zuni and Hopi—silverwork on bracelets. Animals associated with tribal clans were also depicted; examples include badgers and bears.

(l.) Heavy triple silver wire twist shank bangle with five oval blue turquoise stones, c. 1935–1950; (r.) interesting early silver twist ingot bangle, c. 1910. Courtesy of Joan Caballero.

Early ingot silver snake bracelet with stamp work and rocker engraving decoration, 1890–1910. Courtesy of Robert Bauver.

Detail of the snake bracelet.

Early twentieth-century silver cuff stamped with Spanish-influenced floral design, signed on back. Courtesy of Robert Bauver.

Detail of back.

Two Navajo filed and chased ingot silver cast bracelets with natural green Cerrillos turquoise, showing chiseled lines on side of center decoration and on filed plate, first quarter of twentieth century. Courtesy of Karen Sires.

Two ingot silver deep repoussé cuffs, c. 1900. Courtesy of Karen Sires.

Row bracelet set with Hubbell glass, 1920–1930. Courtesy of Karen Sires.

We know that the Knifewing and Rainbow Man deities began to appear in the late 1920s into the 1930s. Stylized *Yei* figures appeared after 1930. Native artisans were—and still are—reluctant to depict exact images of their sacred spirits, fearing the disapproval of medicine men and elders. When possible, dancers with masks would take the place of actual deities, and this worked well with curio jewelry designs. To this day, sacred spirits are shown representationally, and artists are careful not to give away important details when reproducing such figures.

Three classic style bracelets, c. 1900–1915. Courtesy of Karen Sires.

Two cast bracelets with light green stones and exuberant designs from the 1920s. Courtesy of Karen Sires.

Two ingot silver green single-stone bracelets showing heart shape and stamping, 1920s. Courtesy of Karen Sires.

Therefore, smiths put forward such figures cautiously, choosing clowns like the *koshare* and *Koyemshi*. Corn maidens, dancers, and the soon-to-be stereotypical Kokopelli figure started appearing at the end of this historic period. Two kachinas that can be seen in the 1930s are the Long Horn kachina *Sayatasha* and the Blue Horn kachina *Sayathlia*. The examples of petroglyphs and pictographs in the region also gave Native artists a frame of reference for human and animal figures. Navajo and Pueblo smiths created images of the Apache Mountain Spirit (*Gan*) dancer, although these designs appeared more frequently after 1940. The prevalence of spiritual figure designs, however, is still a vintage-era development, rather than one deeply rooted in the historic era.

Creating a "Traditional" Style

Tradition is prized by most Native peoples, especially since their customs have been under steady attack from the dominant mainstream culture. Today, many contemporary Indian artists are uneasy with terminology related to how traditional an art form or style may be. This is largely because of the long-running non-Native practice of seeing older Indian arts as somehow more realistic, true-to-life, or worthwhile. Native artists are rightly concerned that they not be frozen in time in terms of creative ability.

Nevertheless, the literature of Indian jewelry, especially in the hands of anthropologists, had no qualms about defining traditional design and styles. Bracelets often received close analysis. The best example of this is in the exhaustive cataloging of older bracelet forms by Harry P. Mera of the Santa Fe Laboratory of Anthropology. He created a set of brochure-like bulletins for his museum's silverwork collection that included six categories of bracelets and two sections on wrist guards. Much of his work was gathered posthumously by a local publisher, Dale Stuart King, into one volume that appeared in 1960. King followed with a related volume in 1976 that pronounced Mera's findings as authoritative.

Both Mera and King were anxious to define what constituted traditional designs, especially those that might derive from other older arts like pottery and weaving. Their concern was shaped by the freewheeling origins of Indian designs promoted by the commercial curio industry. Mera's examination of Laboratory of Anthropology bracelets dates to the mid-1940s, and he admits to finding post-1930s design suspicious, due to the pernicious nature of commercialism. His categories for separating Indian bracelets by form are invaluable for evaluating technique and decoration. Many collectors date their historical era bracelets on the basis of the photographs in his work.

Mera mentions dates for his photographed examples when he has a firm provenance, although some dates represent when a piece was purchased. His images include cuffs that had been filed and stamped, then embossed, including repoussé work; cast bracelets; carinated forms; wire bands; and "Zuni-style" bracelets. Each of these forms

Three cuffs showing variations on the row bracelet style, 1900–1930. Courtesy of Karen Sires.

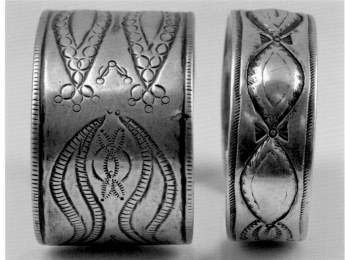

Two Pueblo-made early stamped bracelets, both with repoussé, c. 1900. Courtesy of Laura Anderson.

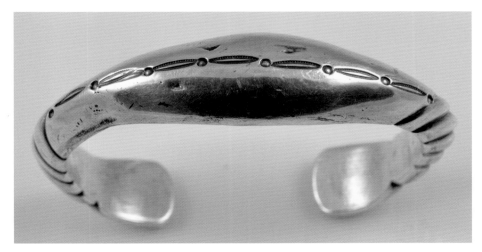

Cast, stamped, and filed bangle with unusually expanded center, 1920s–1930s. Courtesy of Robert Bauver.

Detail: Terminals of two Navajo bracelets with experimental low-domed raindrops; both bracelets show much wear. 1920s. Courtesy of Laura Anderson.

Three-stone hammered coin silver cuff with wedges to support bezel, set with Persian turquoise enhanced by Prussian blue paint, 1920s; originally owned by Laurance Rockefeller and sold in 2005. Courtesy of Ken Wolf.

include bracelets with stones. An overall impression from the Mera book is of mass; many cuffs look heavy. While Mera attributes a date of early 1930s for Zuni-style multiple stonework, it's fascinating to note that this section's examples look as heavy as anything else he shows. King's later book claims that the Zuni practice of using small stones in jewelry-making was a "centuries-old habit."

Other writers established definitions for traditional jewelry forms and design in the 1930s. A 1932 article in *El Palacio* mentions shaped bands, twisted wire employed as designs, and flat sheet silver bands in varying widths as common—implying traditional—in terms of execution (Neumann, 105). Writing in *The Kiva* in 1937, Gertrude Hill lists copper and brass as being the first practice pieces for Navajo smiths, and this holds true for Santo Domingo smiths as well.

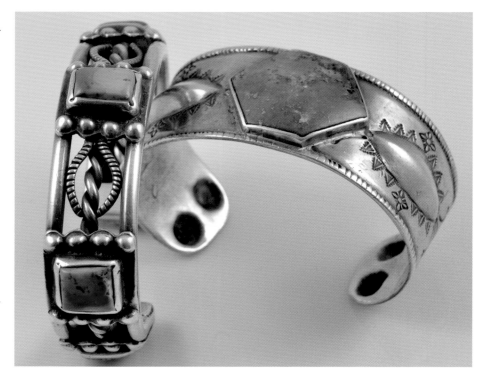

Two green stone bracelets, one (r.) with inventive repoussé and stamping, early 1900s. Courtesy of Michael Horsley.

Three older bracelets: carinated cuff with Carico Lake; 1920s row bracelet; and wide band attributed to Austin Wilson, 1930s. Courtesy of Doug and Kris Sill Collection.

She cites narrow hammered bands with triangular cross-section, broad flat bands marked by single or double strands of heavy twisted wire, and narrow flat bands with stamping as the "more common types" (Hill, 18). She notes that cast bracelets were rarer, but praises them as fine and original in execution.

These same writers, along with others of their time, decried the effects of commercialism in diluting traditional Indian jewelry. Neumann's article derides the manufactured dies used on "pieces made for the white trade" as being "often idiotic …" (Neumann, 105). Hill ends her 1937 article with a warning: "Unfortunately, in the last few years the art of the Navajo silversmith has been sadly debased by the pressure of commercialism …" (Hill, 20). In the rush to establish traditional styles for Southwestern Native smiths and jewelers, this early literature on the subject overlooked exactly how useful commercial practices could be for the evolving bracelet form. To be fair, however, it helps to realize that these writers were more concerned with the ethnographic nature of jewelry production.

Many people find pre-1930 bracelets to be remarkable. One serious collector of historic era jewelry speaks about a certain "lyric" quality that can be seen in the surface decoration. He feels that the whole bracelet was made in a process of creative flow, whereby any slight craft flaws or imperfections act as exclamation marks in an otherwise expressive activity.

CHAPTER FOUR

COMMERCIAL BRACELETS: THE IMPACT OF CONSUMERISM

Certain types of generic Indian bracelets reflect commercial influence in their construction and design. The most radical examples are seen in early to mid-twentieth century trade catalogs of objects mass-produced in factories outside the region. In the Southwest, curio entrepreneurs began looking out for bracelets that would appeal to tourists. Non-Native individuals who established themselves as traders to the Navajo and other peoples might or might not consider commercial practices in their encouragement of the smiths who worked with them. Often, "commercialism" was a dirty word for those in the Indian arts business. Yet Indian traders occupied a key economic role in some locations, such as Zuni Pueblo, with results that helped shape bracelet design during much of the vintage era of 1930–1980.

How did commercial influence affect the designs on bracelets? In accordance with mass and bench production, bracelets appeared more symmetrical. Repetitive decoration was another popular feature. Actual design motifs assume a more overt aspect, in which stylized "Indian" objects, such as crossed arrows and sun faces, become the focus of the bracelet's patterning. More subtle commercial influences developed by midcentury when traders began looking for ideal types of design to encourage and considered the effects of fashion and department store sales. This trend coincided with the rise of the first individualist Native jewelry-makers.

A curio market for Indian arts was already active in the Intermountain West and Southwest by the 1880s (Batkin, vii). The first wave of commercialization of Native jewelry began in earnest around 1895 with the entry of the Fred Harvey Company into Southwestern tourism as vendors and suppliers for the Atchison, Topeka, and Santa Fe Railway. By 1905, jewelry manufacturers in such diverse locations as California, Denver, Chicago and New York became interested in the sales potential of Indian-made jewelry for the tourist trade.

Tourist-era long cuff with green stone, stamp work, and appliqué, 1940s. Courtesy of Vicki Turbeville.

Brass cuff with chip inlay design, Navajo or Pueblo, late 1940s–1950s. Courtesy of Allan and Joyce Niederman Collection.

Group of tourist-era bracelets with picture stone and petrified wood, 1930s–1940s. Courtesy of Paul and Valerie Piazza.

Two tourist-era bracelets: (top) three multiple clusters; (bottom) single-stone with stamping and wire appliqué. Courtesy of Steve and Mary Delzio, The Mexican Shack.

Those who have blamed non-Indians for the design alterations made at this time overlook a significant fact. Instead of being ruthlessly coerced into altering their designs, many Native smiths chose to work for the curio and tourist trade, where they produced adornment that gave patrons and customers what they wanted, learned useful facts about their craft and business practices, and slipped design impulses into an artisanal mode.

Unfortunately, the second wave of commercialism around 1920 confirmed ongoing forgery, misrepresentation, and items called "Indian-made" that were anything but made by Natives. A permanent subcategory of Indian adornment became an economic reality that was cheap, rife with false materials and bogus decorative "symbols." Even today, low-end tourist shops continue to reinforce such negative impressions. None of this was helpful to Native jewelry-makers in the Southwest, faced with tourists who had grown accustomed to low prices.

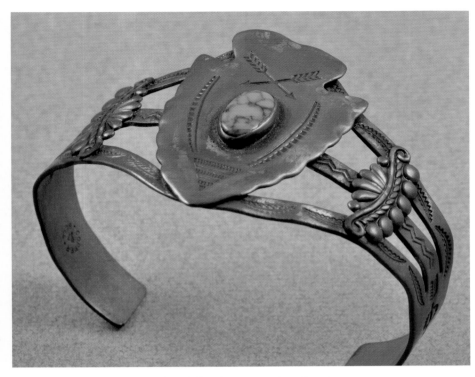

Copper generic arrowhead design bracelet bought at Desert View, Grand Canyon, concession, 1980s. Done in the style of Bell Trading Company copper jewelry from the 1930s. Private Collection.

Stamp of Maisels of Albuquerque, mid-twentieth century. Private Collection.

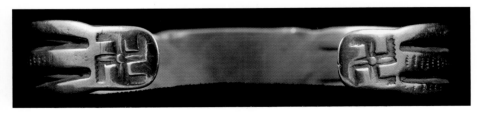

Hand-cut and hammered bracelet design with swastika (or whirling logs), not commercially made but showing commercial influence, 1920s. Courtesy of Philip Bacon Collection.

Nevertheless, Native smiths couldn't depend on sales to fellow Natives alone, and therefore needed to appeal to the non-Native consumer. Curio store operators and middlemen sought compliant Native smiths who wanted work and steady pay. These establishments, confident that they understood Anglo tourist tastes, developed a sense of patronage toward their Indian suppliers, and felt free to dictate design ideas that would boost sales. As early as 1905, it seems Fred Harvey Company official John Frederick Huckel did not appreciate smiths who appeared too entrepreneurial or uncontrolled (Batkin, 115). Those who made commercial jewelry were placed in situations where their design impulses were curbed or altered. Later, however, popular designs could be turned to Native advantage.

By the 1930s, the United States was in the grip of the Great Depression, and Southwestern Indians were struggling with government restrictions on livestock. John Collier's reforms, meant to increase grazing quality on the reservations, left a bad taste in Native mouths. Making silver provided an alternative to failing crops and reduced sheep herds. This was a time when Indians were buffeted by experts preaching assimilation, government officials calling for termination, and a prevailing belief that the American Indian would not survive for many more generations.

The climate was ripe for the encouragement of "traditional" designs, including those for bracelets, and these nostalgic types of works won favor at the region's two newly established Indian arts shows in Santa Fe and Gallup. Non-Native patrons wanted "traditional" Indian arts to be preserved in some manner. Preservation of Indian culture became the watchword for anthropologists and curators concerned with Native-made

Close-up of commercial curio bracelet with swastika stamps, pre-1940. Courtesy of Andrew Muñana Collection.

(l.) Zuni Knifewing design bracelet by Horace Iule, 1935–1945; (r.) cast kachina piece added by C.G. Wallace to a Navajo silver bracelet, 1940s. Courtesy of Eason Eige Collection, Albuquerque, NM.

Matched cast cuffs by Juan Dedios with turquoise, 1920s–1930s. Courtesy of Michael Horsley.

design. They were horrified by the commercialization of Indian jewelry. Led by condemnations from Arthur Woodward, their reproaches can be heard in publications of the 1930s and on. They felt that the purity of Native design was under assault from the tourist trade. Santa Fe museum curator Harry P. Mera loudly decried "the evils of commercialism."

Commercialized "Indian-made" designs brought Indians into the greater popular-culture consciousness by mid-century. Unfortunately, the generic nature of such designs was preferred by tourists to those hand-wrought by an individual smith. Inevitably, when the Native artisan's backlash to craft commercialism set in during the 1970s and early 1980s, this reaction moved jewelry-makers decisively toward fine craftsmanship and individual artistry.

Economic Incentive

The bracelet was already the most popular jewelry form; it was in demand by both Native and non-Native consumers, encouraged by Indian traders, and made more money per piece than other types of adornment. Curio dealers regularly

Nine silver commercial curio bracelets with swastika stamps, all pre-1940. Courtesy of Andrew Muñana Collection.

Commercial ingot silver bracelet with hammered center, swastika design with crude arrows, and gold-plated Knifewing at each end, mid-twentieth century. Courtesy of Andrew Muñana Collection.

Two tufa cast silver cuffs with turquoise mosaic, by Sedelio Fidel Lovato, Santo Domingo Pueblo, 1960s. Courtesy of Joan Caballero.

sought bracelets for their stock. Bracelets were also not particularly difficult to make, save for some forms of tufa casting. The Native silversmiths of the Southwest learned to progress in their craft when economic incentives worked in their favor. Indians located close to the cities of Gallup, Albuquerque, and Santa Fe experienced a stronger pull to work for curio shops and well-established businesses. Those located further away on the reservations took their cues from the Indian traders they chose to work with. Makers and purveyors viewed silver jewelry piecework as a commodity.

Most Indian smiths worked for "the man" in the early twentieth century; they looked to the shop dealer or trader to set prices, supply materials, and sell the work they produced. Those who labored as silversmiths in shops certainly learned much about business. By the 1930s, however, others (such as the U.S. government) sought forms of protectionism for Indian artisans. Their motivations were idealistic, and they did force Indians employed in curio shops into thinking about how to better make a living out of their work. Veterans returning from World War II were less passive than their

Two channel inlay Navajo bracelets, may show influence of traders Tom and Mike Kirk who encouraged this trend, c. 1950s. Courtesy of Joan Caballero.

elders; anthropologists would say they'd become more "acculturated." Soon, the stage was set for new means of combining commercial profit with Indian-controlled metalwork.

No surprise, then, that these Native artists also dreamed of owning shops where they regulated the process of designing and making Native-made jewelry. One of the most successful of these ventures was the Chief Dodge operation where people could find

"quality jewelry direct from the Indians." Located in Tempe, Arizona, this family-owned business promoted an environment where the customer could be part of the entire process, from choosing a desired design to watching the piece being made. Chief Dodge encouraged collectors to eliminate middlemen in favor of buying from an Indian. A 1995 brochure listed such diverse customers as Barry Goldwater, President Reagan, and Liberace! (Heard Archives).

Two turquoise cuffs bought from C.G. Wallace Collection: (l.) Red Mountain carved turquoise on cuff, c. 1950; (r.) butterfly cluster in #8 turquoise, c. 1950. Courtesy of Abby Kent Flythe.

Verso of incised cuff, showing "Handmade at the Indian Garden of the Gods-Colo." stamp.

Two lightweight silver commercial cuffs; one cuff (r.) has commercial thunderbirds and steer head hallmark, other cuff (l., incised) is stamped on verso, 1930s–1940s. Private Collection.

The transfer of economic power from the curio shop owner and Indian trader to the gallery owner and Native artist would be almost complete by the end of the 1980s. The author remembers setting out on extensive road trips through the Navajo Reservation in the late 1980s, only to discover that most trading posts there no longer offered a viable range of jewelry. Some trading posts were in the process of transforming into Indian arts galleries; other traders were relocating to regional cities, and bracelets seemed to sell best in urban locations. In other words, the ethnographic nature of Indian jewelry-making was disappearing, since tourist sales could not sustain the industry. The steady incursion of fake Indian goods, including jewelry replete with plastic block turquoise, phony chip inlay, and designs blatantly taken from Native jewelry shown at the big Indian art markets, continued to be a worrisome issue.

Navajo solid silver bracelet with lighter and more commercial hammering, stamping, and repoussé; signed by David Talliman and marked "Handmade by Indians", 1940s. Courtesy of Karen Sires.

Thunderbird bracelet in commercial style, stamped and hammered, 1930s–1940s. Private Collection.

Lightweight silver tourist-era piece with applied snakes and commercial stamps, 1930s. Courtesy of Karen Sires.

Tourist-era bracelet with swastika (whirling logs) and crossed arrows design, stamped "Hand Made at the Indian Garden of the Gods – Colo," 1920s. Courtesy of Karen Sires.

Verso of bracelet, showing the Garden of the Gods stamp.

So where did the economic incentive to protect quality genuine Indian jewelry—and bracelets—come from? Hopi maintained its Guild standards. The Navajo Arts and Crafts Enterprise had a sometimes bumpy road, depending on its managers, but it remained a source for fairly traditional jewelry designs. Zuni's tribal enterprise ran strong at the pueblo before shuttering its doors in the early 2000s. State laws in the Southwest managed to take down some violators of authentic work, but for every victory in the court there seemed to be yet another backroom operation from Mexico or the Pacific Rim busy at work.

The creation of ethically bound groups, like the Indian Arts and Crafts Association, allowed Natives to become members and have a say in the direction of Indian arts authenticity. This didn't mean that art patronage was over, but those committed to making, buying, and selling Indian arts needed to unite against an enemy that could be found locally or abroad. Native artists watched in anger as individuals sought to photograph the jewelry in their booths at SWAIA Indian Market and other venues, knowing that successful attempts would result in illegal knockoffs of their original designs.

High-end ingot silver tourist bracelet with repoussé by Maisels, and featured in their catalog; considered a classic style, 1930s. Courtesy of Karen Sires.

Slightly asymmetrical ingot silver cuff, filed and chased, with turquoise and jet settings, and stamped scallop by Roger Skeet Sr., c. 1932-1938. Courtesy of Karen Sires.

Trader Influence

From the days of Lorenzo Hubble and C.N. Cotton, Indian traders had a great impact on Indian-made jewelry, largely because they acted as "midwives" or middlemen. They single-handedly created the necessary conditions for Indian smiths to develop their craft and increase sales. The traditional trading post of the early to mid-twentieth century operated as a local resource, allowing Natives to do their banking (including pawning)

with someone they knew and trusted. Bad traders didn't last long, but the process was always based on an old-fashioned patronage role, finally outmoded, once the U.S. became a consumer credit society. As long as reservations remained, the trading post was a useful center; but it became more a place for mail pickups, gasoline, and a convenience store than a shop for fine Indian arts.

Many traders were good American businesspeople. Hubbell, Cotton, and others exported Indian arts and encour-

aged local craftspeople. Since the souvenir market was a limited one, better situated in a regional town or city, mid-century traders sought an alternative market and decided on the custom jewelry trade for department stores and clothing shops. They even went so far as to urge Native jewelers to think in terms of seasonal wear. When turquoise and coral supplies grew low, they imported new materials like Australian opal and semiprecious stones from newly opened mines.

There is no doubt that some of the finest vintage era Navajo and Zuni work was influenced by traders. Indian traders set themselves up as arbiters of taste and good aesthetics for the smiths they worked with. A look at newspapers, especially the *Gallup Independent*, shows that many traders sought prizes for their booth displays at the Gallup Inter-Tribal Ceremonial every August. In fact, when the award-winning work of many Native workers was announced during the 1940s through 1960s, emphasis was placed on the trader who commissioned the work rather than the actual maker. In many cases, traders attempted to react to what they saw as consumer preferences, resulting in short-lived trends, like large-scale bracelets or bracelets with fashionable colors.

Pawn was a problematic matter. Active pawn couldn't be ethically sold if there was a chance the owner wanted to redeem the piece, but dead pawn was fair game. After a while, it became easy to put pawn tags on pieces, especially if they were older or more worn looking. These tags are still around, but consumers need to be wary about the genuine age and value of bracelets marked with such tags.

In the 1970s, the long-standing role of Indian traders as bankers and property handlers came into disfavor; this included their role as middlemen. Hearings were held around the Navajo reservation, in Gallup and Window Rock and other locations, and Indians poured out their displeasure to the authorities. If the times were changing, then so must the Indian trader transform to meet the new era (Baxter, 2000, 82).

Change they did, switching their focus to becoming gallery dealers, suppliers of quality materials for artists, and making their middleman status more congenial. Good traders adopted a different role as a bridge between artists and customers.

This meant that they worked now to establish a best price for artists' works and to advise them on how to draw business. They acted as suppliers looking out for necessary materials for the artists they represented. With the high-end market fully active by the late 1970s, this often meant finding viable turquoise cabochons from a vetted mine, purchasing gemstones, or encouraging (even stoking) a customer's desire for a gold bracelet cuff. Patronage was less critical than partnership.

In the meantime, artists grew stronger in their business identities. Commercial now meant commerce. This didn't mean that all jewelry-makers broke away from some sort of middleman, but they could now act like other mainstream jewelers in terms of business control and outreach. Indian arts shows, however, still represented the most immediate showcase for Native talent and reaching new collectors.

C.G. Wallace and Zuni

Zuni Pueblo, in western New Mexico near the Arizona border, was more isolated than the Rio Grande pueblos. This pueblo, however, received more than its fair share of attention from non-Natives: anthropologists James and Matilda Stevenson studied the Zunis, and that most intrusive of observers, ethnologist Frank Hamilton Cushing, "went native" there. Cushing's accounts of Zuni culture piqued interest in a people who would have preferred more privacy.

From the start, the Zunis proved irresistible to outsiders, especially in terms of the arts. Zuni pottery, beadwork, fetish carving, and jewelry attracted collectors. Zuni lapidary work was particularly enticing. By the early twentieth century, Anglo traders drifted into the pueblo or

settled nearby. They noted that a remarkably large proportion of the inhabitants possessed craft talent, and jewelry-making families created specific designs with collectible appeal.

Zuni artists had some unusual advantages on their side. They made humorous animal and figural designs for use in their craft work, adapted thunderbird and sun face decoration and, by the 1920s, made charming inlay representations of the Knifewing and Rainbow Man sacred spirits. Zuni designs with mosaic and channel inlay were in vogue by 1955, and artisans created small-scale silverwork that Indian traders felt would be popular for sale to tourists and the non-Native market.

Zuni attracted good quality Indian traders and their families: Kirks, Kelseys, Kennedys, Vanderwagens, and Winfields, among others. Nevertheless, one trader in particular would eclipse these other traders' sway in Zuni. C.G. Wallace, a keen businessman and excellent promoter, with strong ties to the Albuquerque curio trade, became the best-known and most outspoken advocate of Zuni jewelry artistry. His take on Zuni artists and their work would influence—and define—the field through the last quarter of the twentieth century and into the twenty-first.

Wallace's pronouncements became accepted as writ to collectors and students of Zuni silverwork. The 1975 sale of his personal collection, documented in a Sotheby's auction sales catalogue, established a strong provenance for key works on the market, including many bracelets. Wallace employed artists whom he began promoting for their individual talent at just the right time in the mid-twentieth century. To this day, an item from the C.G. Wallace collection carries a distinctive cachet. Fine older pieces

Detail of tourist-era bracelet, set with green turquoise and small whirling logs stamp on end, mid-twentieth century. Courtesy of Territorial Indian Arts.

This trader-influenced bracelet was fabricated by a Navajo smith; Veronica Poblano recognizes the abalone, coral, jet, and turquoise inlay Indian Maiden design as an early work of her father Leo Poblano, 1920s–1930s. Courtesy of Andrew Muñana Collection.

Verso of Chief Dodge bracelet.

Silver and turquoise curio bracelet made at and purchased from Chief Dodge shop in Tempe, Arizona, 1970s. Courtesy of Allan and Joyce Niederman Collection.

collected by Wallace are also the backbone of strong silverwork holdings in the Heard Museum and other institutions (Slaney, 52).

Thanks to Wallace, remarkable Zuni artists like Teddy Weahke, Leekya Deyuse, Horace Iule, Dan Simplicio, Leo Poblano, John Gordon Leak (Robert Leekity?), and Frank Vacit are big names in the historic and vintage Indian arts market. Yet, like any other older businessman and collector who led an active life, Wallace made small mistakes, generalizations, and simplifications in his recollections; nonetheless, his infallibility was so trumpeted by those writing about Indian arts that his words received virtual canonization. A good example of this can be found in Dale Stuart King's *Indian Silver Vol. 2* (1976). In a section on jewelry motifs, he writes of "… C.G. Wallace, the greatest living authority on the history of Indian silver" (King, 59). Wallace's aesthetic leadership was further cemented in later publications and a groundbreaking exhibition at the Heard Museum in 1998.

Wallace wanted Zuni jewelry to have a strong identity of its own. To aid this endeavor, he began emphasizing Zuni small-scale lapidary genius, and took pains to distinguish Zuni aesthetic elements from other elements in Navajo and Hopi work. He used Navajo silversmiths who lived in the Zuni area, and often spoke of collaborations between Navajo smiths and Zuni lapidaries; yet many of these collaborations were motivated by Wallace's own financial considerations. Nor did this concept originate from Wallace. Indian traders often dealt in piecework and used lapidaries who happened to be Zuni, setting their stones in silver shaped by Navajo smiths.

Inlay work grew more popular and technically sophisticated due to tools introduced after the 1940s, and Wallace credited his Zuni artists for this development. The use of small stones was economically practical and paralleled the Native taste for cluster work. Wallace encouraged needlepoint, petit point, and channel inlay, and claimed this work as part of Zuni "style." The winning aspect of Zuni figural designs was echoed in playful carved animals, insects, and human and kachina forms that blossomed on cuffs. Zuni bracelets were sometimes made as sets, pairing the central cuff design with one on a bolo or a buckle.

The notion that Zuni was a "village of silversmiths" took root. Where Wallace led, other traders followed and expanded upon his tenets. Certainly, collectors began enjoying the extended family nature

Long cuff with two turquoise stones and four bear claws, mid-twentieth century. Courtesy of Allan and Joyce Niederman Collection.

Two Zuni inlay bracelets (l. to r.): butterfly design and Knifewing figure, possibly by Dan Simplicio Sr. Courtesy of Karen Sires.

Group of children's bracelets, 1940s–1950s. Courtesy of Paul and Valerie Piazza.

Butterfly cuff inlaid with abalone, jet, turquoise, coral; and narrow band turquoise and jet inlay on silver, both by Lambert Homer, Zuni, 1940s–1950s. Courtesy of Abby Kent Flythe.

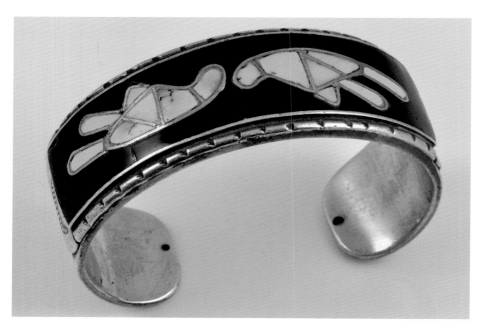

Mid-twentieth-century example of Zuni Knife-wing design bracelet colored for fashion purposes. Author's Collection.

Parrot inlay bracelet attributed to Lambert Homer Jr., c. 1950s, formerly in C.G. Wallace catalogue. Courtesy of Laura Anderson.

of Zuni artistic genius, and books about Zuni artists reinforced the idea of family-owned designs and styles. What people understood less, though, was that Zuni ideas about intellectual property and design ownership were more fluid than Wallace and other purveyors made them out to be. An individual might be known to create a certain design, such as a thunderbird or corn maiden, but that didn't preclude a family member from setting the design in metal or producing the item in the artist's name. A sister or son might make the actual piece, especially if the usual maker was ill or occupied with tribal or religious obligations, but the item could still be sold in the name of the artist associated with its conception.

To counter this reality, Wallace and other traders insisted on hallmarks. Things still proved to be a bit more elastic. Zuni tribal names, including multiple branches of a family, might prove to be confusingly similar. (The same can be said of Santo Domingo pueblo jewelry-makers in the mid-twentieth century.) However, Zuni's Indian traders began pushing the naming of individual artists, and identifying specific families as the holders of various design and decorative motifs. Confusion

Zuni three-row bracelet with rectangular stones and double raindrop ends, 1940s–1950s. Courtesy of Robert Bauver.

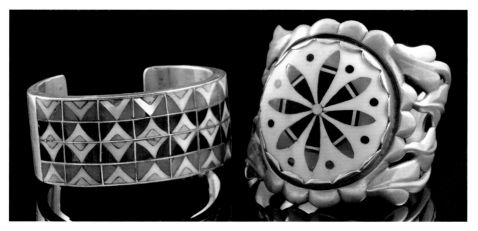

Inlay and abalone Zuni bracelets, 1950s–1960s. Courtesy of Karen Sires.

Two playful Zuni bracelets with inlaid round faces, makers unknown, 1920s–1930s. Courtesy of Andrew Muñana Collection.

Dan Simplicio Sr. cuffs with Mediterranean branch coral and turquoise, 1940–1960. Courtesy of Karen Sires.

This unusual thunderbird bracelet design was a collaboration between Frank Vacit and Dan Simplicio Sr., 1940s–1950s. Courtesy of Andrew Muñana Collection.

and innocent misdirection inevitably arose. New evidence in oral history documentation is beginning to overturn some previous assumptions that C.G. Wallace made authoritative. While Zunis rightfully claim expertise in lapidary work, they also prove to be more experienced in silvercraft than previously thought.

Collectors need to know that historic and vintage era Zuni bracelets, like other jewelry forms of the times, are the product of very specific social conditions and attitudes. Zuni, always a conservative pueblo, was open to interpretation by non-Natives who lived and worked in proximity with its peoples. Sometimes these individuals, including Wallace, didn't always get the story completely straight.

Bracelets are among the stars in the Wallace Collection auction catalogue. There, one can see the array of midcentury styles, traditional in nature but most definitely not "classic." Wallace retained works from major Navajo smiths like Roger Skeet, John Hoxie, and Austin Wilson. Pictures of bracelets by Zuni artists also show great similarities to Navajo silverwork. Nevertheless, the quality of small-cut stones, for channel, cluster, needlepoint, and figural designs, by artists like Annie Quam, Dishta, Oliver Cellicion, Warren Ondelacy, and Jerry Watson are outstanding. One jeweler shines out in particular in the catalogue: bracelet designs by Dan Simplicio Sr. foreshadow the creative artistry of the 1970s and beyond.

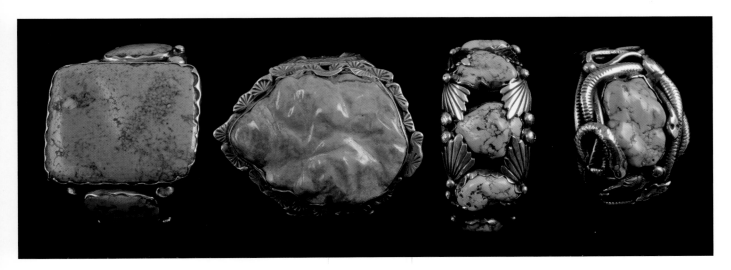

Four turquoise carved bracelets by Dan Simplicio Sr., 1940–60. Courtesy of Karen Sires.

CHAPTER FIVE

The iconography of the American Indian was established in public consciousness by the 1930s, according to cultural historians (Engber, 2013, 21). From the early U.S. penny to sports team logos, an Indian shown in profile became an iconic design element. So too at this time did the sheer volume of Southwestern Indian geometric designs impress itself on mainstream public perception. Aesthetically, the timing couldn't be better. American decorative tastes during the 1930s veered to art deco and machine age designs that complemented Southwestern Indian patterning.

Native work in this spirit received its greatest artistic affirmation in the 1941 "Indian Arts of the United States" exhibition at the Museum of Modern Art in New York. The curators, Frederic Douglas and René D'Harnoncourt, intended to elevate Indian arts to a new level. They displayed examples of Southwestern Indian craft as fine art objects imbued with an ethnic sensibility parallel to early modernism. Some of this attribution may have been motivated by patriotism: with Europe in the midst of war, Americana was an alternative offered to those hungry for art.

The exhibition catalog furthered this agenda by describing Southwestern Indian metalwork—and Navajo designs in particular—as having "forms derived from a variety of sources." When describing Navajo silver, including a photograph of a wide cuff anchored with a large square turquoise stone, the authors mention stamps or dies as being "…for decoration only and have no symbolic significance" (Douglas, 133). Equally interesting is the adoption of an exhibition section entitled "Living Traditions" (Douglas, 115).

Indian-made bracelets evolved in four key directions during the fifty years of the vintage era. Each of these directions arose from developments that occurred in the face of increasing modernization. In addition, these changes laid the groundwork for the transition from craft to art. The first new direction allowed makers, purveyors, and consumers to define traditional design and create a classic style that celebrated what had come before; it set the basis for what would become known as old-style design. The second direction, which peaked through the 1950s and 1960s, saw the creation of silver bracelets that emphasized first-rate and dramatically shaped turquoise from Southwestern regional mines. A third direction ensued when smiths began to render the curio aesthetic into an innovative folk style. The fourth, and most pervasive, direction began when Native makers experimented with design and style that led to genuine individualistic artistry.

Classic Style

Where and why did the term "classic style" originate for Indian bracelets?

In fine art, the term for classical Greek art indicated a historical period where artistic design, quality, and execution were considered superb, as opposed to the less skilled art of the previous archaic and later Hellenistic periods. Ancient Greek and Roman creations were considered high art; this belief was instilled through the educational system followed by Western civilization. The term "classic" or "classical" slipped into usage to denote high-quality design based on earlier examples, and experts on Southwestern Indian arts now revived these terms to apply to designs they considered most genuinely Native in concept and execution.

The bracelet cuff was an ancient adornment form known to the Greeks and Romans. Museum curators and experts of the 1930s and 1940s began applying the labels "classic" and "classic style" to early Indian jewelry examples when this jewelry was receiving its first true scholarly

1950s cast Navajo bracelet. Courtesy of Albuquerque Museum, Eason Eige Collection.

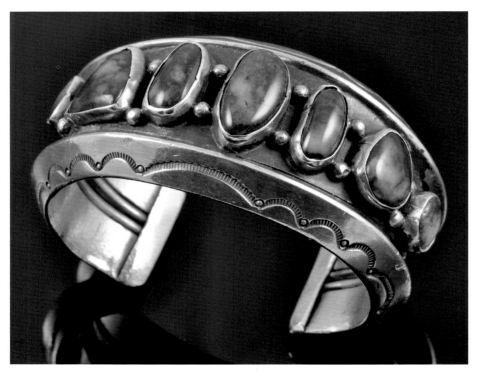

Wide cuff with high-grade Bisbee turquoise stones by Mark Chee, 1960s. Courtesy of Doug and Kris Sill Collection.

attention. These experts' assessments were picked up by traders and dealers, passed on to consumers, and accepted by Native artists who found such definitions useful.

In fact, the use of "classic style" as a term supports the notion of a living art. It presupposes a greater antiquity for Native metal jewelry-making than is actually the case. Yet this was not the sole intention of those who labeled certain cuff styles as being classic. These individuals were concerned about preventing the adulteration of older design through commercial influences. The "false" adaptations of the curio trade provided a threat to the making of a truly classic style of jewelry, especially bracelet cuffs.

Dr. Harry P. Mera of the Laboratory of Anthropology in Santa Fe fired the first salvo in the war against commercialized

Cast cuff set with #8 turquoise containing brown matrix, 1950s. Courtesy of Vicki Turbeville.

Verso showing drop-in seal.

Indian jewelry. He published brochures of examples in the Laboratory's collection as a means of setting standards and defining what constitutes "good" craftsmanship. His reverence for nineteenth-century

creations, along with the stronger and better examples of the early twentieth century, was made clear. He applauded older, strongly rendered cuffs that were geometrically symmetrical in nature.

Mera included pieces with punch work and repoussé as fine examples of classical design. He praised bracelets containing symmetry and balance. Geometric and abstract patterns were

Three "traditional style" cuffs by Mark Chee, 1950–1960s. Courtesy of Michael Horsley.

Silver cuff by master smith Austin Wilson, 1940s. Courtesy of Michael Horsley.

Cuff with large turquoise stone and stamps marked "U.S. Navajo 2" on back, c. 1938–1942. Courtesy of Michael Horsley.

Austin Wilson made this three-stone turquoise bracelet engraved "1935" and "K.W." (possibly for his sister Katherine). Courtesy of Martha Hopkins Struever.

Butterfly cluster cuff with Lone Mountain turquoise, 1930s. Courtesy of Laura Anderson.

Bracelet set with carved turquoise frogs by Leekya Deyuse, 1920s–1930s. Courtesy of Michael Horsley.

Three-stone turquoise and silver bracelet with good side design, 1940s. Courtesy of Vicki Turbeville.

elements that can be visually traced to classic style sources.

Today, any bracelet—no matter when it was created—may be judged to be classic style if it fulfills the requirements of being modeled on older design and decoration, is well-proportioned, possesses clean metalwork and finish, and is technically flawless. Nowadays, most post-1980 Native jewelers refuse to be locked into an either/or creative definition that derives from design critics. Instead, many of today's bracelet makers will tell you that they incorporate classic style features only when they wish to do so. Design freedom is one of the options contemporary Native artists prize most.

Skystone and Silver

An excellent introduction to traditional and newly artistic intentions appeared in 1976 with the publication of *Skystone and Silver: The Collector's Book of Southwest Indian Jewelry* by Carl Rosnek and Joseph Stacey. This book went out of print fairly quickly and became a highly

clearly favored over figural designs. And Mera condemned anything that looked commercial. His conclusions were taken up with enthusiasm by Arthur Woodward, John Adair, and others.

This author wishes to offer for consideration the idea that the definition of classical designs as applied to Indian bracelets did not end at the year 1930. In fact, classic style came into being between 1920 and 1960, when those

who had learned from the first generations of Indian smiths now made similar designs using improved tools to achieve a stronger, cleaner visual effect. Looking at Indian bracelets as a whole, "classic style" came to mean a style of design devised by older generation smiths and better executed by those who emulated their intentions. As early as the 1980s, Native smiths began calling these designs "old-style," and they most often feature design desirable (and expensive) title on the secondhand book market in the 1980s and 1990s. Filled with remarkable photographs, this work shaped collector expectations about Indian jewelry. All forms of Native-made jewelry received attention in the book, including bracelets.

The visual point made best here lay in the depictions of Indian bracelets inlaid with high-grade quality turquoise, coral, and shell—the traditional "stones" of choice for the Native maker. *Skystone and Silver* helped to create the collector craze for good turquoise and depicted the silver and stone bracelet as the ultimate treasure. Many dealers in the Indian arts business acknowledge that this book served as the educational primer for serious turquoise adornment collectors. The book's depiction of 1950s and 1960s vintage era cuffs had a remarkable impact on both Native jewelry makers and bracelet collectors.

Silver bracelets set with stones received collector attention, helped by the fact that many mines opened for the first time in the 1940s and later, including a number in Nevada. The reality, however, was that Southwestern regional mines opened and closed with regularity as promising veins were tapped out. Collectors and enthusiasts of turquoise developed aesthetic tastes for quality stones. Certain mines also assumed their own classic status: Lone Mountain, Bisbee, Morenci, and others. Even repurposed stones possessed value. Many a canny Native smith began amassing high-grade turquoise from various mines to use in current—and future—creations. Since turquoise cabs could be shaped in attractive ways, bracelets began appearing with remarkable jewel-like center stones. Multiple stone cuffs also proliferated through the 1950s, including cluster work bracelets that suited Native tastes. By the 1970s, many turquoise mines were closing with alarming frequency.

The importance of Indian bracelets can be seen during the 1960s. The Scottsdale National Indian Arts Exhibition

Five-inch-long cuff with Zuni Knifewing design, 1950s. Courtesy of Vicki Turbeville.

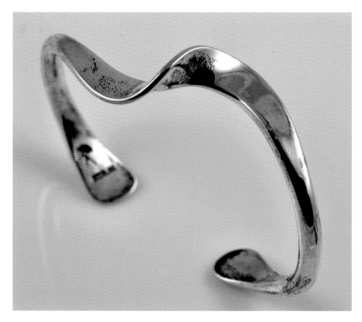

Unusually shaped bangle by Tony Aguilar, 1950s. Private Collection.

Twisted bangle in heavy-gauge silver by Randy Hoskie, post-1980. Courtesy of Norman L. Sandfield.

Five bracelets set with petrified wood, 1930s–1940s.
Courtesy of Vicki Turbeville.

Non-commercial-made small, heavy bangle, set with central turquoise stone,
while two other stones are bottle glass, possible experimental stamp designs,
1930s. Courtesy of Philip Bacon Collection.

Heavyweight cast piece with green stone,
1940s–1950s. Courtesy of Vicki Turbeville.

An early link bracelet made with Kingman turquoise, 1950s.
Courtesy of Paul and Valerie Piazza.

Two Hopi cuffs, one with Kingman turquoise, 1940s.
Courtesy of Paul and Valerie Piazza.

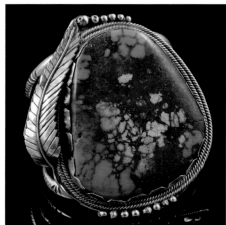

Large triple-shank cuff with oversize stone and raindrops decreasing in size, hallmark stamp by Ha-Hu-Ya, 1960s. Courtesy of Eason Eige Collection, Albuquerque, NM.

Double-ridged cuff made from two bands of filed stamped ingot silver joined at the terminals, and a center plate, 1940s–1950s. Courtesy of Philip Bacon Collection.

Hopi cuff with twisted wire and geometric overlay by Paul Saufkie, Hopi, late 1940s. Courtesy of Michael Horsley.

Group of cuffs with stones, mid-1930s–1950s. Courtesy of Eason Eige Collection, Albuquerque, NM.

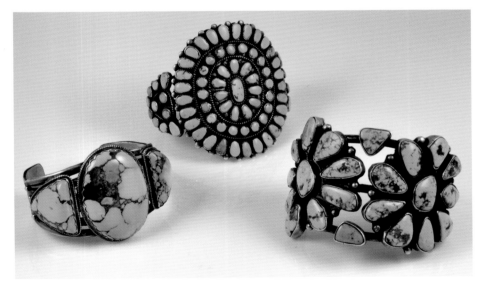

started awarding prizes to jewelers in 1964. That year, the first prize went to Joseph Alvarez for a cast silver bracelet, and another bracelet, by Charles Chee Long, won honorable mention. In 1965, Joe Quintana won first place for a turquoise and silver bracelet. Another skystone and silver cuff made by George Nez won an award in 1969. The California Palace of the Legion of Honor in San Francisco held the exhibition *Southwest Indian Arts II* in 1965. The catalog for the exhibition featured three styles of Indian bracelets: a silver bracelet and pin set by Kenneth Begay with a classic scroll design, an anonymous maker Zuni silver bracelet set with needlepoint turquoise, and a Hopi-made overlay cuff lent by the Hopi Silvercraft Cooperative Guild.

Silver bracelet set with petrified wood by Ralph Tawangyaouma, Hopi, 1940s. Courtesy of Michael Horsley.

Back of bracelet, showing hallmark.

Innovation

Popular culture of the mid- to late 1960s produced some interesting variations on the commercial Indian bracelet. The 1960s marketplace received an influx of watchband bracelets and decorative watchband tips (tips are not illustrated in this book). While this jewelry form originated from commercial sources, it surpassed many curio pieces in popularity as a type of masculine fashion. Southwestern men appreciated its regional connotations. Link bracelets were another curio-inspired form. The influence of hippie culture inspired the rather ridiculous "slave bracelet" that consisted of a band with a chain extending from the cuff to a ring that matched the bracelet's design. A good number of bracelets from this time used inexpensive materials like chip inlay.

The growing strength of the Native American Church introduced designs meant to honor its rituals. The peyote bird and peyote bud drew from existing thunderbird and circular motifs. Many

Navajo or Pueblo hollow silver bracelet with channel inlay, 1950s. Courtesy of Bill and Minnie Malone.

Heavy-gauge wide cuff with mosaic inlay by Charles Loloma, 1960s. Courtesy of Janie Kasarjian Collection.

Silver cuff with Morenci turquoise and onyx by Preston Monongye, 1960s. Courtesy of Waddell Trading Company.

Cluster bracelet set with Lone Mountain turquoise, 1960s. Courtesy of Bill and Minnie Malone.

Classic style cuff with Persian turquoise by Kenneth Begay, 1960s. Courtesy of Janie Kasarjian Collection.

Ten Mark Chee bracelets, with two unusually narrow bangles, showing his versatility, 1950s. Courtesy of Joan Caballero.

Three tufa cast silver Navajo Guild bracelets, 1935–1950. Courtesy of Joan Caballero.

Two 3½-inch silver cuffs with turquoise by Preston Monongye, c. 1961–1962. Courtesy of Abby Kent Flythe.

Southwestern Native men served in the Korean and Vietnam conflicts and returned to seek healing in the Church's rites. Designs like these became more popular with Native men, and can be seen most often on watchbands, masculine cuffs and rings, and bolo slides.

Indian traders sought to capitalize on a relatively brief trend toward making large-scale jewelry—the larger the better. The results of this trend appear baroque and rather fantastical. We can admire these pieces after the fact, but the short duration of such production is indicator enough of their lack of success. Jewelers went through a period of creative innovation that headed in various directions, and even down some blind alleys. Such innovations of the 1950s

Cast bracelet set with Godber turquoise, early 1960s. Courtesy of Abby Kent Flythe.

Cuff with carved turquoise and coral by Emerson Bill, 1970s. Courtesy of Abby Kent Flythe.

Cuff with four-inch oval Blue Gem turquoise with strap across stone (possibly to hide a crack), leaves on outside, 1960s. Courtesy of Abby Kent Flythe.

Large cuff with gem quality Blue Diamond turquoise and fine stamping, by George Kee, 1960s. Courtesy of Abby Kent Flythe.

Classic style piece of Zuni-made cluster made for Native market with original pawn tag from 1960 (showing a price of $24). Courtesy of Robert Bauver.

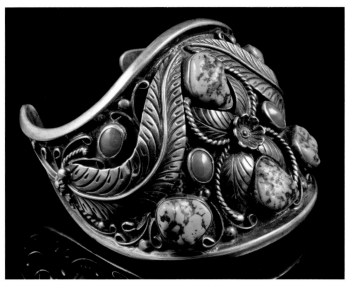

Commercialized popular leaf design of 1970s, with turquoise and coral nugget cabochons, "LA" hallmark. Courtesy of Steve and Mary Delzio, The Mexican Shack.

1970s chip inlay: (l.) peyote bird design on watchband, signed "B. Ben" on back; (r.) cuff with coral and turquoise. Courtesy of Steve and Mary Delzio, The Mexican Shack.

and 1960s, however, were significant steps on the way to individualistic design.

Fashion was a useful direction, and at this time Indian smiths and traders began considering how Indian jewelry could be marketed as valid costume jewelry. Lloyd Kiva New, an innovative Native fashion designer, ran a shop in Scottsdale during the 1950s. He collaborated with Charles Loloma and others on fashionable accessories, like woven handbags with metal ornamentation. Ethnic design became "chic" in this time period.

Experimentation

By the 1960s and 1970s, Southwestern smiths had access to better equipment and training with Native or non-Native jewelers. Master smiths like Kenneth Begay, Morris Robinson, Horace Iule, Frank Vacit, and Tony Aguilar drew inspiration from both their own heritage and the mainstream accomplishments that made aspects of the metalcraft so enjoyable, such as cuttlefish casting and reticulation. While the White Hogan was one of the better-known workshops for creative collaborations, young

Detail of Effie Calaveza snake bracelet, her trademark design, 1970s. Courtesy of Steve and Mary Delzio, The Mexican Shack.

Frank Patania Sr. classic cuff with lapis stones, c. 1940s–1950s. Courtesy of Doug and Kris Sill Collection.

Cuff with three stones by Morris Robinson from 1950s. Courtesy of Karen Sires.

Hopi overlay cuff with parrot design in heavy-gauge silver, 1970s. Courtesy of Steve and Mary Delzio, The Mexican Shack.

Wide cuff by Mark Chee with strong stamps, 1940s. Courtesy of Karen Sires.

Two cluster bracelets (l.) 1930s; (r.) 1940s. Courtesy of Karen Sires.

Two silver bracelets by Ralph Tawangyaouma, 1940s–1950s. Courtesy of Karen Sires.

Cluster bracelet and single stone cuff by Ralph Tawangyaouma, 1940s–1950s. Courtesy of Karen Sires.

Natives worked with experienced jewelers at other nearby establishments. Non-Natives like Frank Patania and Pierre Touraine helped many youthful artists get a start in the jewelry industry. More Indians attended regional colleges, which opened up the world to them.

Experimentation also meant working with new materials not previous considered "traditional." Learning to be a fine jeweler involved handling gold, diamonds, and even gemstones. Just as Charles Loloma's career soared in the 1960s, so did a path appear that led to the start of a genuine high-end market for Indian-made artistic adornment. Wondrous bracelets began to appear in newspapers, magazines, and the windows of upscale galleries.

Fine-quality materials were crucial to such creations. Even inlay lapidary work, generally limited in the past to turquoise, coral, and shell, expanded now to take in opals, pearls and unusual semiprecious stones. While the cuff shape still dominated bracelet forms, the band would be tweaked to better highlight the ingenuity of the jeweler. Many jewelers listened when Loloma—an expert marketer well aware of the power of fashion—suggested they create cuffs that

Overlay bracelet by Victor Coochytewa, Hopi, 1950s–1960s. Courtesy of Karen Sires.

Two bracelets: three-stone bracelet, 1940, and wide silver cuff, 1950s, by Austin Wilson. Courtesy of Karen Sires.

Silver bracelet by Navajo master smith and jewelry instructor Ambrose Roanhorse, 1940s. Courtesy of Karen Sires.

"U.S. Navajo 60" wide cuff from Santa Fe Indian School, and narrow bangle marked "U.S. Zuni 1," both c. 1938–1942. Courtesy of Karen Sires.

Five solid silver and stone set Navajo Guild bracelets, 1940s–1960s. Courtesy of Karen Sires.

Three Juan Dedios bracelets with animal designs and wonderful terminals, 1930s–1940s. Courtesy of Karen Sires.

enhanced the wearer. Ironwood and ivory entered the repertoire of smiths, no longer limited to the turquoise and silver palette. Another trend at the end of the vintage era was a propensity for pairing turquoise and coral on bracelets, rings, and pendants.

Even those smiths who worked in non-urban settings caught the fever for experimentation. For bracelets, these ventures most often had to do with size, scale, and proportion of decoration. Some experiments did not produce an aesthetically pleasing result, and it's interesting to see these failed efforts when they pop up on the marketplace. Smiths who pursued classic styles at this time benefited from improved stamps. The effective use of shadowbox also marks the latter half of the vintage era. Silversmiths showed a new interest in using oxidation for

*Lone Mountain turquoise set bracelet by Fred
Peshlakai, 1940s. Courtesy of Karen Sires.*

contrast, particularly on the center band and terminal areas of the cuff. Figural designs increased in the 1950s through 1970s, some more successful than others.

Experimentation served as a good social indicator of the increasing acculturation of Indian jewelers in the Southwest. Individualists exposed to a steady barrage of outside influences, from college to television, now looked at design in new ways. Some jewelers enjoyed their work, investing creations with a playful aspect. By the end of the 1970s, more books with Indian jewelry designs were available to provide inspiration. Indian jewelers could look at examples collected from the past or admire contemporary pieces that hinted at the future to come.

CHAPTER SIX

MOMENT IN HISTORY: 1970s BRACELETS

The 1970s was the decade when American Indian jewelry "suddenly" came into vogue. Stories vary on exactly when and how this transpired, but there is strong informal agreement from those active in the field at this time that conditions in the early 1970s encouraged more Native men and women to become silversmiths. Publications from the mid-decade also mention renewed interest in Indian jewelry. For example, in a special issue of *Arizona Highways* from 1975, one writer alluded to a recent jewelry boom, claiming prices for pieces had tripled over the last three years (Stacey, 71).

We also know the 1970s as the decade when America began to embrace its ethnic diversity more fully. Change had been building for some time. Social protest, rage, and upheaval marked the turbulent 1960s. College students and others agitated for a more inclusive society. While many Indian families, especially those in remote reservation areas or still living in a pueblo, chose to remain traditional in lifestyle, more Natives were living off-reservation and in regional towns and cities than ever before. As they were wired for electricity, more and more Indian homes had televisions; the "window on the world" promised to American housewives also brought that world to Native viewers.

A Charles Loloma stepped-stones bracelet of the early 1970s. Courtesy of Waddell Trading Company.

Cast silver bracelet with natural Nevada turquoise by Preston Monongye, early 1970s. Private Collection.

Large cuff set with Mediterranean coral, 1970s. Courtesy of Vicki Turbeville.

Heavy-gauge silver Zuni cuff with inlaid turquoise, onyx, mother of pearl, and coral bead, 1970s. Courtesy of Vicki Turbeville.

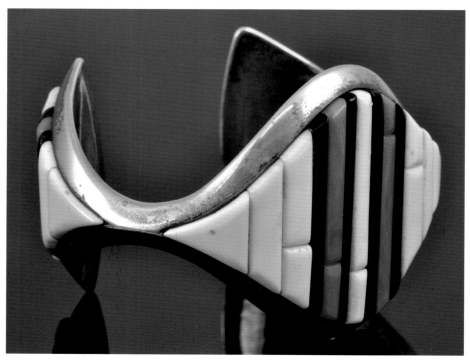

Gold with diamonds bracelet by Victor Coochytewa, late 1970s. Courtesy of Funny Company.

Cuff with fossil ivory, coral, and onyx, incised signature "Dawsa," 1970s. Courtesy of Vicki Turbeville.

The movement we now call inter-tribalism took shape in this decade. Labeled "pan-Indianism" at the time, it called for a closer union between all Indian peoples. For art, this movement took expression through the Institute of American Indian Arts (IAIA) established in Santa Fe in the 1960s. Young Native artists from all over the U.S. and

Canada brought their visual heritage to this special two-year college (now a four-year institution). Art students learned from each other, and design was enriched by new motifs and forms of patterning. Artists not from the Southwest also found the region's Indian arts shows in Arizona and New Mexico helpful to their careers.

Mainstream popular culture appreciation of ethnic arts blossomed at this time. The Indian jewelry "boom," whatever it was, convinced a healthy number of youthful Southwestern Indians to make a career from such work.

Indian trading posts became the subject of a backlash movement and Federal Trade Commission investigation. Hearings were held and abuses in the pawn system reported. Some pawning would continue, but Indian jewelry ceased to be a viable trade commodity. Change was in the air, although it would take until the 1980s before the industry outgrew its craft status and took on the aspect of decorative *art*.

If we want to find evidence of the bracelet's expanded role at this time, we need look no further than the remarkable number of books produced on Indian jewelry in this decade. They provided a wealth of visual documentation. The writers' commentaries drew from scholarly, collector, and popular culture sources, and while an ethnographic tone and anthropological perspective still prevailed, most authors acknowledged they were treating an active, living craft.

Biases displayed in these books created long-lasting effects. For example, following Adair's lead, Navajo jewelry, including bracelets, captured the most attention, leaving Pueblo creativity to a few specialized studies. From this point on, Navajo jewelry, simply by being more plentiful, eclipsed the work of all other Southwestern tribes. In many publications, "Navajo" often becomes a substitute term for all Native jewelry.

Looking back on this development, it's difficult not to conclude that this was simply a matter of numbers and economic clout. While the Santa Fe Indian Market offered a balanced overview of contemporary Southwestern Indian jewelry, with the various pueblos well represented, this was offset by the Navajo-centric Gallup Inter-Tribal Ceremonial and its trader sponsors. Museum professionals borrowed from the tribal style trends of the period; the Zuni, Hopi, and Navajo marketplace festivals held at the Museum of Northern Arizona attempted to emphasize tribal craft distinctions.

Literature with an ethnographic focus that appeared in the 1970s helped those

Stepped-stones bracelet with jade, Lone Mountain turquoise, ironwood, and ivory by Charles Loloma, 1970s. Courtesy of Funny Company.

Lone Mountain turquoise and silver bracelet by Mark Chee, late 1970s. Courtesy of Funny Company.

who wanted to know the visual design characteristics of older Indian jewelry. Arthur Woodward's *Navajo Silver*, originally based on a Museum of Northern Arizona bulletin of 1938, was published as a book in 1971; bracelets fared well in this publication. His investigation of pre-1930 bracelets made distinctions between early Navajo bangles and cuffs, Eastern and Plains bracelets with designs borrowed by Navajo smiths, and analysis of Spanish and Mexican decorative influence. He had his own prejudices; he felt that the "overabundant" use of turquoise on rings and bracelets was bad and even "garish" (Woodward, 59).

The decade saw the creation of an authoritative publication by Margaret Wright, *Hopi Silver* (1972). This study also drew from resources of the Museum of Northern Arizona, which had a history of supporting Hopi art as early as the 1930s. Wright's book helped ascertain key artists, hallmarks, and designs, and revealed the historic breakaway from heavy Navajo-like silverwork to the overlay technique that Hopi artists rendered brilliantly. Bracelets feature prominently in this book, along with a keen understanding of Hopi design control, aesthetic assurance, and how their guild work made their creations so well-defined.

No equally relevant literature appeared yet for the Rio Grande pueblos. In many cases, the research needed for such studies was almost insurmountable, especially for Isleta and Santo Domingo pueblos, rich in bead and silver artistry. Zuni was brought into the picture through C.G. Wallace's 1975 auction and sales catalogue. Interestingly, two collector-based publications of the decade stressed Zuni's complex web of artist families. Ed and Barbara Bell, dealers from Grants, New Mexico, self-published *Zuni: The Art and the People* (1975–77) in three slim volumes. The Bells' photographs

Spider with web cuff by Preston Monongye, mid-1970s. Courtesy of Paul and Valerie Piazza.

Storyteller cuff by Clarence Lee, 1978. Courtesy of Paul and Valerie Piazza.

Wide tufa cast cuff with yellow shell, coral, and turquoise inlay by Preston Monongye, 1970s. Courtesy of Michael Horsley.

Two cuffs, one tufa cast and other with Blue Gem turquoise, by master jeweler Preston Monongye, 1970s. Courtesy of Janie Kasarjian Collection.

and text show the work of individuals, along with husband/wife and parent/child teams. The same focus appears in dealer Gordon Levy's *Who's Who in Zuni Jewelry* (1980), a tantalizing snapshot of images with a "1970s" feel, showing pieces that are fairly commercial in repetitive design and execution.

A more significant publication, Margery Bedinger's *Indian Silver: Navajo and Pueblo Jewelers*, emerged in 1973 from the University of New Mexico Press. This was a scholarly codifying of Adair's classic *Navajo and Pueblo Silversmiths* (1944), with an endorsement of Mera's and Woodward's findings. The similarities in focus to Adair are no mistake, especially in terms of the very limited review of pueblo silversmith efforts, and this key book firmly declares the dominance of Navajo jewelry over other Southwestern tribal jewelry-making. If anything, this book verifies the popular culture assumption that Navajo silverwork was *the* premiere form of Southwestern Indian jewelry.

Bedinger's comments on the bracelet form echo the work of the earlier ethnologists, but she had original points to make about the aesthetics of the silverwork. Interestingly, her ideas reinforce the concept of "classic" bracelet design, although she never uses this word in her text. She endowed Navajo silverwork with "five basic senses," or aesthetic qualities that reflect cultural spirituality, and used bracelets as illustrations. These characteristics are: "strength, simplicity, proportion, contrast, and symmetrical balance" (Bedinger, 106-7).

While most 1970s authors focused on Navajo silverwork, in the marketplace vintage era Pueblo jewelers were proving to be innovative makers of bracelets. Victor Coochwytewa and Paul Saufkie of Hopi; Joe Quintana of Cochiti; and Antonio and Dominic Duran, along with Tony Aguilar

Cuff with Lander turquoise, made before being dealer influenced, by Lee Yazzie, 1976. Courtesy of Janie Kasarjian Collection.

14K gold cluster bracelet by Alice Quam, pre-1980. Courtesy of Bill and Minnie Malone.

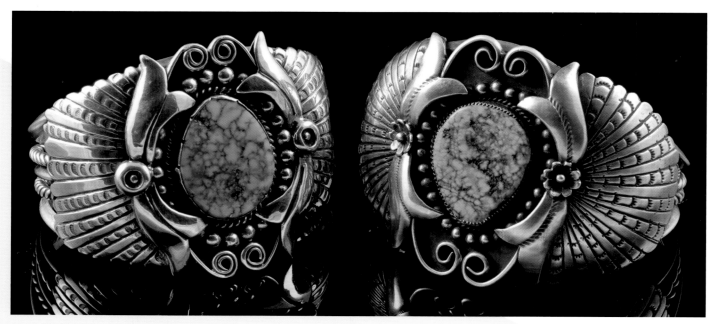

Two cuffs with squash blossom design in Morenci turquoise by Minnie Malone, mid-1970s. Courtesy of Bill and Minnie Malone.

Six brass bangles by Leo Coriz, Santo Domingo Pueblo, 1970s. Courtesy of Joan Caballero.

Cuff set with Lavender Pit Bisbee by Johnny Pablo, early 1970s. Courtesy of Abby Kent Flythe.

Large cuff set with high-grade Kingman, 1970s. Courtesy of Bill and Minnie Malone.

and Julian Lovato of Santo Domingo, contributed plenty of skilled bracelet designs.

The end of the vintage era saw the merger of innovation and experimentation as individualist artists trumped the piecework artisan. Hallmarks became the rule and not the exception. A significant number of Southwestern Indian artists broke out at this time—and they had things to say and points to make. The instructors and students of the IAIA had more than a decade of collaborative incentive. Creative inter-tribal solidarity boosted artists' design consciousness and aesthetic boundaries. Consumers and collectors proved receptive.

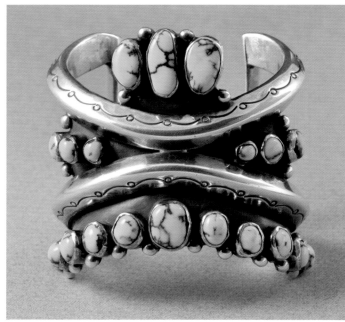

Bracelet set with Spiderweb Bisbee by unknown maker, 1970s. Courtesy of Abby Kent Flythe.

Bracelet measuring 3½ inches with "KB" hallmark by Kenneth Begay, 1970s. Courtesy of Abby Kent Flythe.

Lone Mountain web turquoise cuff by Lee Yazzie, late 1970s. Courtesy of Abby Kent Flythe.

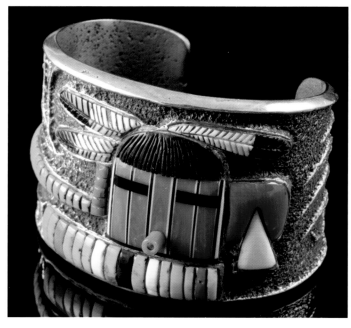

This cuff, showing the "Laguna Gambler" kachina face with jaclas, was a collaboration between Preston and Jesse Monongye in 1975. Courtesy of Abby Kent Flythe.

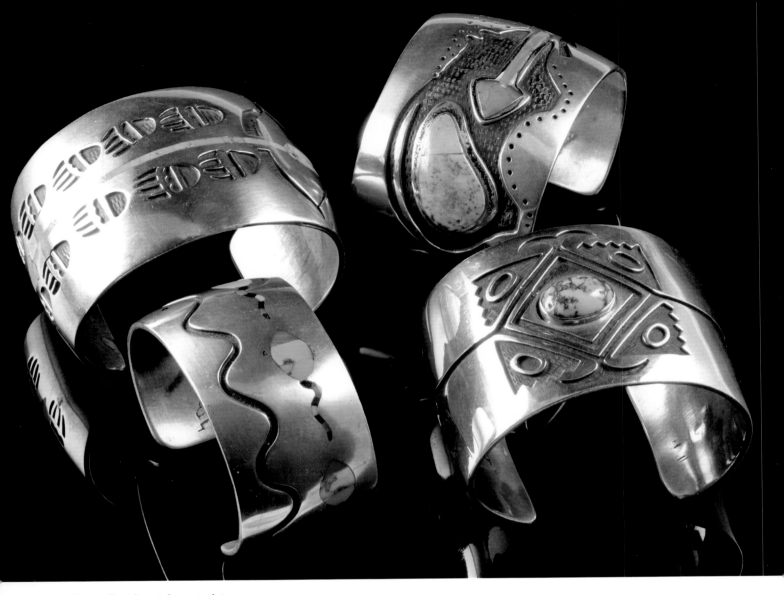

Group of four cuffs with varied organic designs by Manuel Hoyungva, Hopi, 1970s. Courtesy of Abby Kent Flythe.

Black inlay squared silver cuff marked "Jesse's Creations" by Jesse Monongye, 1975–1976. Courtesy of Abby Kent Flythe.

A dark shadow over this era, however, was the arrival in the marketplace of pirated designs and an added spate of bogus, unsuccessful works that harmed the reputation of genuine quality jewelry. Cheap chip inlay "hippie bracelets" and lackluster commercial cuffs (including wide copper cuffs with inlaid arrowheads) warped consumer expectations. An intriguing book titled *Indian Jewelry: Fact & Fantasy* was published in 1976; the author was motivated by worries over the "fad" nature of 1970s creations (Lund, 5).

"Boom" or not, the decade created conditions that encouraged Native jewelers in the Southwest to experiment with a natural playfulness that highlighted the idealism of the times. Looking at bracelet styles in a global manner, we can see many similarities between Native American cuffs and bracelets from various regions. African American and Caribbean women now wore stacks of silver bracelets, just as women from India and Pakistan clustered bangles in gold, silver, and inlay materials. Incised silver cuffs from Guam, silver repoussé bangles from Qatar, and Tibetan and

Large 1970s-design cuff with dark turquoise stones by Eddie Begay. Courtesy of Steve and Mary Delzio, The Mexican Shack.

Large cuff with composite design with chip inlay and coral and green turquoise cabochons, stamped "Navajo Handmade," by Richard Begay, 1970s. Courtesy of Steve and Mary Delzio, The Mexican Shack.

Five-strand band cuff, with center band of turquoise heishi beads, possibly by Lura Moses Begay, 1970s. Courtesy of Steve and Mary Delzio, The Mexican Shack.

Persian bands fashioned with silver and turquoise—all bear uncanny resemblances to Navajo and Pueblo silverwork.

The 1970s proved to be the decade when everything came together to ensure the Southwestern Indian bracelet had a multifaceted identity. The concept of the Indian cuff as costume jewelry tied to fashion took hold. Already accepted as a souvenir of a picturesque region, the Indian bracelet could also be viewed as ethnic design, folk art, craft art, and—with the arrival of master jewelers working in high-end materials—fine art.

In 1975, Tony Aguilar's twisted brass bracelets and Domingo Abeyta's cuffs received media attention at Santo Domingo's first Arts and Crafts Fair.

Oversized three-stone turquoise bracelet, possibly Royston, "EN" hallmark, 1970s. Courtesy of Steve and Mary Delzio, The Mexican Shack.

Two large-scale bracelets of the 1970s: one turquoise and silver and one cuff with bright blue turquoise stone and coral cabochons. Courtesy of Steve and Mary Delzio, The Mexican Shack.

Two tufa cast bracelets by Larry Golsh, one (l.) with Morenci turquoise, 1970s. Courtesy of Karen Sires.

Ingot silver cuff with filed and chased patterning and set with Bisbee turquoise by Joe H. Quintana, c. 1975. Courtesy of Karen Sires.

An early silver and turquoise bracelet by Ray Tracey purchased in Gallup in 1978. Photograph by Danny Luwe. Courtesy of Allan and Joyce Niederman Collection.

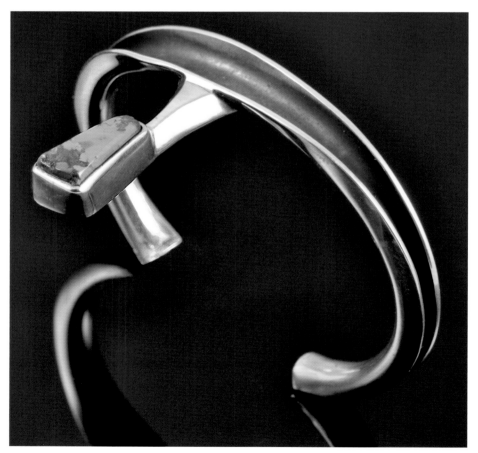

Unusually shaped and deceptively simple Charles Loloma band, oxidized and with turquoise, mid-1970s. Courtesy of Doug and Kris Sill Collection.

In December of that year, an article on Preston Monongye in the *Los Angeles Times* was accompanied by a photo of his "Black Spider Woman" bracelets and mentioned that his work sold for high prices. In March 1975, *Arizona Living* featured an article on Harold and Sedelio Lovato, taking time to describe the fashionable materials they employed to decorate tufa cast bracelets, among other adornment.

The bracelets shown in this chapter give us a real visual sense of the decade. We see, too, the flowering of bracelet styles, including those defined by master innovators. From Charles Loloma's distinctive stepped-stones cuffs to the revival of elegant tufa casting by Larry Golsh, individualistic artistry is evident. Indian humor glints in the silver storyteller compositions of Clarence Lee. Ray Tracey, a 1970s figure who created Navajo designs—many offset by fine inlay— gained numerous fans. A proliferation

Verso of gold bracelet, showing the McGee's stamp.

14K gold bracelet with Blue Gem turquoise, made at and purchased from McGee's Indian Den, Scottsdale, Arizona, 1970s. Courtesy of Allan and Joyce Niederman Collection.

of large stone and cabochon high-grade turquoise bracelets by Lee Yazzie and Johnny Pablo made a strong impact on collectors. The clever father and son collaborations of Preston and Jesse Monongye often featured wide cuffs with center-stage presentation designs meant to ride on the wrist.

Greater emphasis was now placed on luxury, as in the use of gold for bracelet cuffs. As a final accolade, a 1979 issue of *Arizona Highways* included an article on "The New Indian Jewelry" that let Preston Monongye, among others, tell the public what to expect in the future. While the traditional turquoise and silver cuff remained steadfastly "classic," new possibilities were appearing, and the decade's taste for ethnic style made the Indian bracelet very much in vogue.

This timeless fashion appeal impressed designer Ralph Lauren. He came to prize turquoise and silver adornment after

Artistically designed wide cuff with turquoise and wire shaped into organic form, 1970s. Courtesy of Steve and Mary Delzio, The Mexican Shack.

Silver overlay storyteller bracelet with female figures in Monument Valley landscape by Robert Becenti, Jr., 1970s. Courtesy of Steve and Mary Delzio, The Mexican Shack.

Silver cuff with cornrow pen shell and turquoise heishi beads, unknown maker, 1970s. Courtesy of Steve and Mary Delzio, The Mexican Shack.

Wide cuff with wire decoration, heavy-gauge twisted wire in floral pattern on oxidized background, Royston turquoise stone, 1970s. Courtesy of Steve and Mary Delzio, The Mexican Shack.

Composite 1970s bracelet shows questionable design: abalone center with popular design figure of Pueblo woman, but two domed green turquoise stones on side, possibly Zuni. Courtesy of Steve and Mary Delzio, The Mexican Shack.

interactions with inspirational Santa Fe dealer Teal McKibben. Lauren launched an American heritage clothing line in the early 1980s that borrowed from Native weaving, pottery, and decorative metalwork designs. A number of young and rising Native jewelers did piecework for Lauren's company in the 1970s, and they became design leaders over the next several decades (Cirillo, 2008, 34). Nowadays, despite the lapses in aesthetic merit, even uniquely eccentric 1970s Indian-made bracelets are regaining a more respectable vintage sheen.

This cuff's design by Jesse Monongye was the result of an airplane trip he made, inspired by staring down at the landscape's varied surfaces, 1979. Courtesy of Doug and Kris Sill Collection.

CHAPTER SEVEN

NATIVE STYLE: 1980 AND BEYOND

"Fashion represents one of the most basic and compelling of artistic impulses...the art of personal adornment."

—Lloyd Kiva New from *American Indian Fashion from Lloyd Kiva New to Now*. Heard Museum North, Nov. 21, 2013- March 31, 2014.

The 1980s set the tone for a period of national indulgence in luxury. This decade, more than any other time, confirmed a high-end collector market for Indian jewelry that still thrives today—in spite of recession and belt-tightening. Individual artistry became the watchword for exquisitely crafted bracelets. Maisels in Albuquerque and other curio store survivors still produced generic designs, but most silver and turquoise pieces had their maker's hallmark or name stamped on the back. The Gallup Inter-Tribal Ceremonial and Santa Fe Indian Market continued to draw visitors, including a strong core of collectors interested in specific jewelers. Trading posts were closing or morphing into art galleries. The 1980s created a new kind of Indian trader—an individual who worked with Native artists to help sell unique creations in a gallery setting.

These transitions came in the face of continuing practices like steep

Silver cuff with Hopi design by Victor Coochytewa, c. 1990s. Courtesy of Waddell Trading Company.

Two old-style bracelets, one made from coin silver, by Perry Shorty, c. 2010. Courtesy of Waddell Trading Company.

Bracelet with damele and onyx stones by Michael D. Garcia (Na Na Ping), c. 2000. Private Collection.

discounting and suspect materials that gave Indian arts a degraded reputation among the general public. Particularly worrisome was the reality that many of the regional turquoise mines were playing out. Coral and other semiprecious minerals became harder to obtain. During the 1980s, Native jewelers experimented with new materials, from Australian opal to South African sugilite. Indian jewelry enthusiasts and collectors still wanting traditional materials had to be persuaded to give these stones a chance. Gemstones became part of a new look.

Native artists aspiring to high-end status formed partnerships with mine owners opening new veins or dealers who could supply them with cabochons preserved from mines long gone. More and more, gold factored into an artist's creation. Non-Native jeweler Pierre

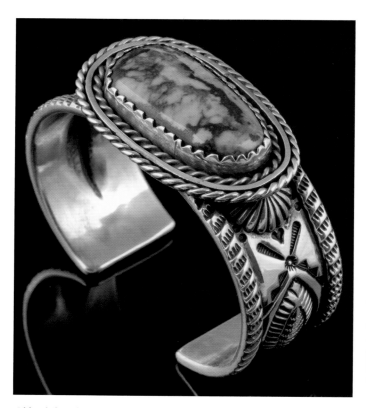

Old-style bracelet with Bisbee stone by Clendon Pete, c. 2007. Private Collection.

Watchband by Gary Reeves, c. 2001. Private Collection.

Touraine, who had worked for Van Cleef & Arpels in Paris and Harry Winston in New York, opened a shop in Scottsdale where Native artists like Larry Golsh and Don Supplee went to draw inspiration and learn how to be more facile with non-traditional materials like diamonds and gold.

Indian arts shows in the 1980s began seeing "best of show" bracelets look anything but old-style. In 1983, the Gallup Inter-Tribal Ceremonial jewelry prize winners were Ray Yazzie with a gold bracelet inlaid with turquoise, lapis, coral, and mother of pearl, and a cuff in gold and silver adorned with cutouts by James Little. The *Indian Trader* reported in October 1987 that a Lee Yazzie intricately inlaid bracelet was retailing for $18,000.

Sophisticated materials allied to more avant-garde cuff designs made the entire

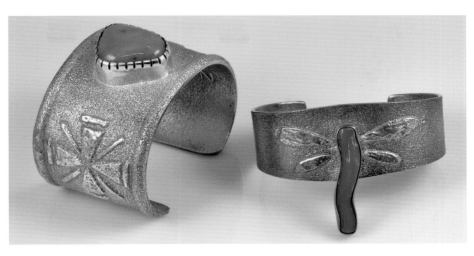

Tufa cast cuffs with coral and dragonfly, by Olin Tsingine, 1990s. Courtesy of Vicki Turbeville.

Three old-style stamped and repoussé silver cuffs by Ernie Lister, c. 2012. Courtesy of Vicki Turbeville.

Silver triple-wire bracelet by Raymond Twinhorse (San Felipe), c. 2000. Private Collection.

Silver and stone bracelet by Lee Yazzie and Lena Henry, 1980s. Courtesy of Stuart W. Early Collection

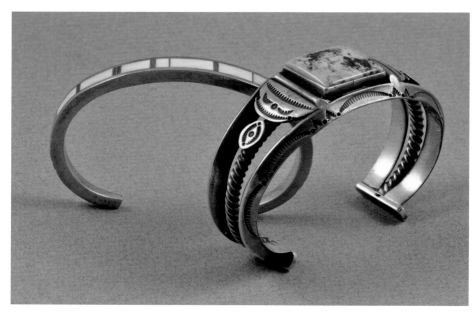

Plain silver cuff showing hallmark by Cippy Crazyhorse, c. 2008. Courtesy of Eason Eige Collection, Albuquerque, NM.

Two bracelets by Ray Tracey showing conventional and inlay styles, 1990s. Courtesy of Paul and Valerie Piazza.

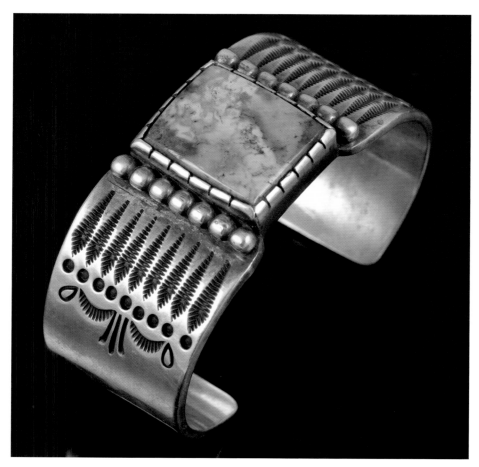

Natural Royston and silver cuff by N. Nez, 2006. Courtesy of Eason Eige Collection, Albuquerque, NM.

ethnic art market stronger after the 1970s. More people began to appreciate adornment from diverse cultures, and the New Age movement displaced the old hippie ethic. New Age whetted an appetite for natural materials with "spiritual" qualities. Fashion in the 1980s, with companies like Chico's and the United Colors of Benetton, produced clothing with multicultural ethnic designs. A September 1989 issue of *Phoenix Home & Garden* devoted pages to "Art to Wear" Native jewelry and fashion.

A growing consumer urge for fine craft objects, work that was artistic in nature, refreshed the status of Indian arts as Americana. Jewelry achieved break-out status in this new celebration of American Craft, and the taste for "wearable art" coincided with a growing trend in Indian arts. In 1986, the American Craft Museum opened in New York (renamed the Museum of Arts and Design in 2002); this institution has staunchly supported Native-made design in exhibitions and publications ever since its inception.

Rolled steel bracelet set with industrial diamonds by Pat Pruitt, Laguna Pueblo, post-1980. Courtesy of Janie Kasarjian Collection.

Bracelet with micro inlay and added diamond by Carl Clark, 2007. Courtesy of Janie Kasarjian Collection.

Charles Loloma inspired those who embraced craft artistry, although they represented an earlier period of active collaborations, just as Lloyd Kiva New awoke young Native interest in the power of fashion. Loloma broke the model of traditional jewelry by introducing new stones and new shapes. By the 1980s, young jewelers and clothing and accessory designers were quick to follow their lead, blasting their way through modernist modes to create the new wearable art.

The proliferation of Indian arts shows and awards through the 1980s helped anchor the success of the Native-made cuff. In addition to his 1983 "Best of Show" at the Gallup Inter-Tribal Ceremonial, Raymond Yazzie won again in 1987 at the Gallup Ceremonial with an intricate inlay bracelet. The 1984 SWAIA Indian Market winners of Division "A" Traditional Jewelry included Edith Tsabetsaye, Roderick Tenorio, Clarence Lee, and Jake Livingston. Four years later, at the 1988 Gallup Ceremonial, the bracelet makers to watch, in terms of awards, were Perry

Artistic cuff with Siberian jade by Richard Chavez, 2011. Courtesy of Janie Kasarjian Collection.

Bracelet with inlay Indian face by Danny Romero,
Yaqui, c. 2005. Courtesy of Abby Kent Flythe.

Two cuffs by Raymond Yazzie, one (l.) with
Mediterranean coral, lapis, and turquoise, 1980s.
Courtesy of Abby Kent Flythe.

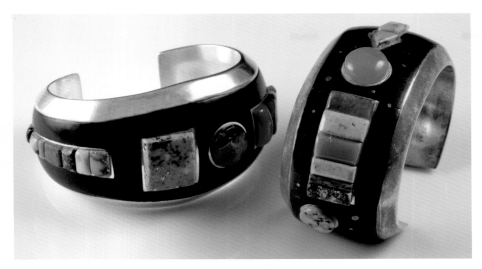

Two silver cuffs with ironwood background and various inlaid stones by Ted Draper, Navajo, c. 2005. Courtesy of Abby Kent Flythe.

This Darryl Dean Begay "Native Woman" bracelet has a turquoise face; it is sitting on a reticulated cuff with one line of inlay, c. 2000–2002. Courtesy of Abby Kent Flythe.

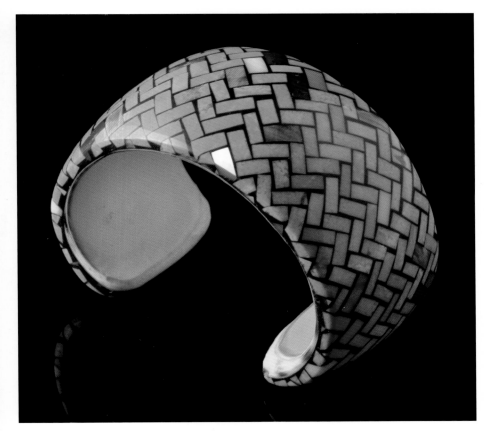

Mosaic on shell cuff by Charlene Reano, Santo Domingo Pueblo, c. 2006–07. Courtesy of Abby Kent Flythe.

Shorty, Edison Smith, Allison Lee, Harlan Coonsis, and Orville Tsinnie.

The 1980s signaled a period when deliberate innovations were making bracelets less traditional in appearance. Watson Honanie, encouraged by trader Bruce McGee of Keams Canyon, began making gold overlay top sheets with cutout designs soldered to a bottom sheet of silver. In April 1982, an article in the *Arizona Republic* carried predictions by dealers that the lack of high-grade turquoise reserves would raise prices for collectors and drive a new search for alternative materials. Old stones soon popped up for reuse in new bracelets where the design was far from conventional. By the 1980s, collectors knew which master innovators to turn to for quality examples of experimentation in action.

The continuing attention to fine art bracelets not made in the old-style surfaced

Four bracelets with good quality turquoise by Michael Roanhorse, c. 2007-8. Courtesy of Abby Kent Flythe.

Turquoise cluster bracelet and ring in design much favored by Native owners, 1980s, "DMT" hallmark. Courtesy of Steve and Mary Delzio, The Mexican Shack.

in the 1990s. A 1991 brochure from the Lovena Ohl Gallery in Scottsdale featured large cuffs by Phil Poseyesva and Richard Tsosie with distinctive overlay designs. The same gallery in 1994 showed a fine gold bracelet with an arrow design enhanced with diamonds by James Little. At the various tribal marketplace shows at the Museum of Northern Arizona in 1998 and 1999, Watson Honanie, Roy Talahaftewa, Tony and Ola Eriacho, Dylan Poblano, Leo Yazzie, Ric Charlie, and Darryl Dean Begay all received awards for their bracelets.

The American Southwest was an attractive marketplace for American Indian jewelers who were not from the region. Jewelers began to share a taste for materials, motifs, and design concepts from tribes of the Plains, Oklahoma, Pacific Northwest,

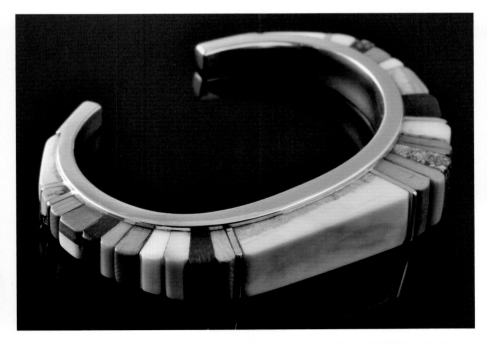

Silver cuff depicting Navajo shepherdess with turquoise sun by Darryl Dean Begay, 2013. Courtesy of Faust Gallery.

Ivory and multiple stones on gold cuff by Sonwai, c. 2000. Courtesy of Faust Gallery.

18K gold cuff with jet and sugilite by Charles Supplee, 1985. Courtesy of Faust Gallery.

Three silver bracelets by Marco Begaye depicting the various styles he works in, 2012–13. Courtesy of Faust Gallery.

or even farther north and east. Along with shared Native identity and new types of materials, Indian artists relished the freedom in design that flourished into the new millennium. Northern Cheyenne designer Ben Nighthorse Campbell (a U.S. Senator until his retirement in 2005), helped sponsor legislation for the National Museum of the American Indian and was honored with an inaugural exhibition of his jewelry when the Museum opened in 2004. Plains-style beading impacted bracelet design in particular. Marcus Amerman, Choctaw artist, has made brilliant beaded masterworks that have wowed collectors. Teri Greeves has also dazzled collectors and critics with her ingenious beadwork, making bracelets that are richly iconic in design.

Three contemporary artists whose works have garnered critical acclaim for

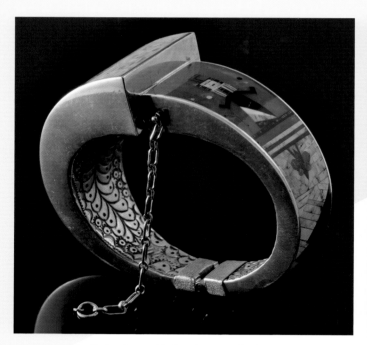

Clasp bracelet by Carl and Irene Clark with micro inlay design, coral, turquoise, jet, and intricately carved silver interior, c. 1980. Courtesy of Faust Gallery.

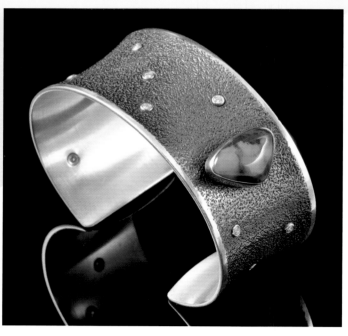

Cuff with industrial diamonds, oxidized surface, and small Bisbee stone by Chris Pruitt, Laguna Pueblo, 2012. Courtesy of Doug and Kris Sill Collection.

Two differently styled cuffs by Victor Beck, one masculine with coral inlay band made c. 2000, the other in a feminine style with coral, jet, ivory, and turquoise oval face, from mid-1970s. Courtesy of Doug and Kris Sill Collection.

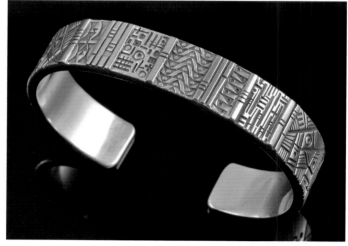

Gold and silver cuff with art deco-like design by Norbert Peshlakai, c. 1997. Courtesy of Doug and Kris Sill Collection.

being forward-looking, especially in terms of bracelet design, are Cody Sanderson and Chris and Pat Pruitt. Sanderson, proud of his Diné heritage, fashions metalwork cuffs and bands with pop culture bounce. Pat and Chris Pruitt, from Laguna Pueblo, have made their metalsmith careers very relevant; their artistry is rooted in tradition even as it may appear unconventional in its resemblance to mainstream and avant-garde ornament. Look more closely, however, and the legacy of the first 100 years of Native metalwork underlies Pat Pruitt's tributes to industrial design in stainless steel. These three artists share an instinctive sense of Native Style. Their designs for bracelets are far from static, suggest movement, and convey interesting plays of light, shadow, texture, and contrast.

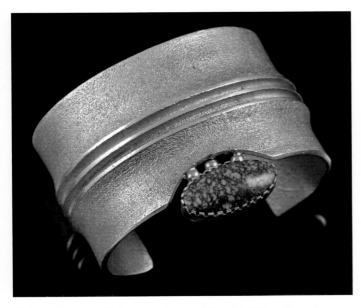

Tufa cast bracelet with fine turquoise in gold bezel by Edison Cummings, c. 2006. Courtesy of Karen Sires.

Hand-hammered and forged repoussé fish design cuff by Liz Wallace, 2010. Courtesy of Karen Sires.

Most Southwestern jewelers make bracelets, but some artists are more active in creating experimental layering variations on the form than others. This chapter can only mention a limited range of cuffs by contemporary makers. One of the most exciting talents today is Liz Wallace, known for her skill in the *plique-a-jour* enamel technique. Individuals who create diverse bracelet designs that enthuse viewers at the annual Indian arts shows are Darryl Dean Begay, Marco Begaye, Mike Bird-Romero, and Sonwai.

The sculptural use of mosaic and other forms of inlay add to the three-dimensional vigor of contemporary cuffs, which become fitting canvases for new artistry. Creatively expressive inlay bracelets are the hallmark of Benson Manygoats, Jesse Monongye, Danny Romero, Raymond Yazzie, and Alvin Yellowhorse. Avant-garde cuff designers of note include Edison Cummings, Michael D. Garcia, Vernon Haskie, and Norbert Peshlakai. Market attention is

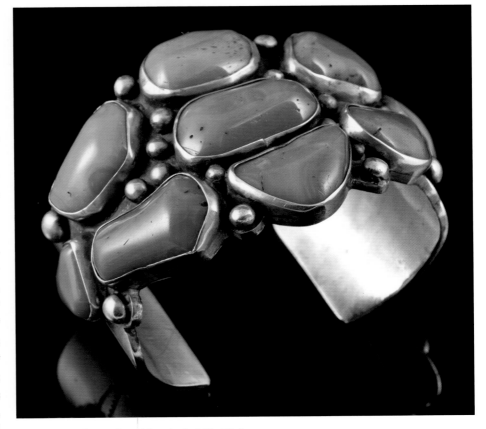

Heavy-gauge silver and coral bracelet by Mike Bird-Romero, 1980. Courtesy of Karen Sires.

Cuff with black inlay night scene by Alvin Yellowhorse, 1980s–1990s. Photograph by Danny Luwe. Courtesy of Allan and Joyce Niederman Collection.

"Review of the Universe" inlay cuff by Jesse Monongye, 1980s. Courtesy of Allan and Joyce Niederman Collection.

Danny Romero link bracelet, 1990s. Courtesy of Allan and Joyce Niederman Collection.

regularly paid to the classic old-style bracelets of Ernie Lister, Perry Shorty, and Orville Tsinnie.

Native Style features in a variety of artistic viewpoints. Particularly noted for their contributions in this mode are the Gaussoin family of artists, including Jerry, David, Wayne Nez, and their talented mother Connie Tsosie Gaussoin. Carlton Jamon and Dylan Poblano from Zuni make cuffs with this resonance. What remains to be seen is how Native Style will flow into the work of the next generations of jewelers, many of whom have trained with the artists mentioned in this book.

The last thirty years of Southwestern Indian cuff design have been enhanced by artistic collaborations, cross-cultural exchanges, and engagement with non-traditional casting and surface patterning techniques. Artists' personal investigations into bracelet fabrication break up any tendencies to make the Indian cuff static in its presentation. Today's Native artists rue the influx of imitation, bogus, misrepresented, and fraudulent jewelry that continues to haunt the marketplace.

What does the Southwestern Indian bracelet mean today as a jewelry form? Most people believe that the ethnic element gives these bracelets its iconic status. But,

if you ask someone to describe such a bracelet, don't be surprised if that person refers to the first hundred years of its creation—and to its skystone and silver qualities. Never mind that today's Native-made bracelet, like a Southwestern Indian ring, can be created with an indefinite combination of materials. In the passage from craft to art, Native Style still runs true.

Therefore, the truth of today's Southwestern Indian bracelet design history is that, while Native artists may look anywhere they like for inspiration, there remains a core reliance on the older cuff form. There have been artists who've experimented with the physical form,

Overlay bracelet with cut-out by Michael Kabotie, 1980s. Courtesy of Laura Anderson.

Beaded cuff bracelet depicting Chief Red Cloud by Marcus Amerman, 2010. Photograph by Danny Luwe. Courtesy of Allan and Joyce Niederman Collection.

Hands designs with strong overlay contrast by A. Honanie. c. 2000. Private Collection.

Silver and single stone bracelet purchased from Julian Lovato at the 1983 Santa Fe Indian Market. Photograph by Danny Luwe. Courtesy of Allan and Joyce Niederman Collection.

but the fundamental aesthetic for such a bracelet still lies in the period between 1870 and 1970.

Look at the bracelets shown in Chapters 1 through 5 and compare them to the creations displayed in this chapter. If you begin to examine the way the newer cuffs appear, you can still see their roots as being traditional and even classic, even when they are not deliberately made to look old-style. Southwestern Indian bracelets have never looked better than now. They've been refined, highlighted, and infused with artistic and cultural cachet. They have multiple identities that are pleasing in their own right.

This positive development can be traced to the bracelet's design origins.

By 1930, transformations in bracelet surface design turned into powerful identifiable motifs. Patterns appeared, linked and recognizable, ready to become conventional ornament. This repertoire of design was made more aesthetically handsome with the addition of improved tools and more malleable sheet silver. After several more decades, such work became a visual archive, or legacy, to be passed down to future generations.

Another key feature born in the early history of the Southwestern Indian bracelet is its sculptural nature. Early cast work emphasized this quality and it remains an aesthetic force throughout subsequent decades. Loloma's stepped-stones bracelet reanimated artistic explorations and collector interest. Post-1980 attention to the sculptural can be found in the playful creations of the Gaussoin family, who added new touches to the cuff shape. Add in the award-winning sculptural variations of Fritz Casuse, visual statements made by Duane Maktima, Sonwai's impact on younger artists, and the organic sculptural inlay of Lyndon Tsosie, and new definitions for Native Style come readily to mind.

Dexter Cirillo, whose documentation of contemporary Southwestern Indian jewelers is extensive, understands that their work has been enriched by this legacy of design motifs. She sees these motifs as cultural references to the Southwestern Native world view of the Navajo and Pueblos. Cirillo's examination of such work over the last thirty years reveals that jewelry motifs, including bracelets, have become more conceptual and narrative in nature. By incorporating representational, abstract, and conceptual design from their cultural history, contemporary Southwestern Indian jewelers are "ensuring the continued evolution of a dynamic art form" (Cirillo, 2009, 69).

Beaded leather bracelet with dragonfly design by Teri Greeves, c. 2008. Private Collection.

Northwest Coast-influenced cuff with carved walrus ivory fish and abalone by Mike Bird-Romero, c. 2004. Courtesy of Martha Hopkins Struever.

Three silver bracelets: wide cuff (on left) from 1980s, others from 1990s, all by McKee Platero. Courtesy of Abby Kent Flythe.

"Points Up High" silver bracelet by Cody Sanderson. Courtesy of Albuquerque Museum, Eason Eige Collection.

Perry Shorty bracelet with stamped sides and double row of turquoise, post-1980. Courtesy of Martha Hopkins Struever.

Silver and turquoise bracelet by Allison Lee, c. 2004. Private Collection.

In this book, we have redefined how traditional and classic styles apply to historical and vintage era bracelets. The social changes of the 1970s, in particular, brought Southwestern Indian bracelets out of a solely ethnic craft context, confirming their status as living art. Native jewelry-making after 1980 also established conditions whereby the artists made clear they controlled what they chose to create. This does not mean art patronage is unwanted or undesired—just that the relationship between maker and buyer has been altered.

In other words, we can return to a truth uncovered in *Southwestern Indian Rings*: Native jewelry-makers have always controlled their designs. They may have been previously instructed, guided, or directed about certain motifs in the past, but their vision is the dominant one.

This means that we need to look for the Native-created motive in this design history analysis of Indian bracelets. Since the story of American Indian jewelry design has always been *their* story after all—not a clever collaboration of mainstream and indigenous vision as earlier writers determined—our evolution in understanding comes about when we see a shared Native creative impulse.

Native curators and writers have begun using a term to explain such an impulse. In the early 2000s, Anishinaabe scholar and writer Gerald Vizenor began defining the concept of **survivance** as a way of changing our understanding of the stories of America's Native peoples. Vizenor argues that non-Natives are too wrapped up in "concocted images of the Indian." Survivance is a merger of the terms "survival" and "resistance." It demonstrates a process of ongoing change that pertains to design as well as words. When applied to Indian jewelry design, its creators move into the future by transforming the past—a

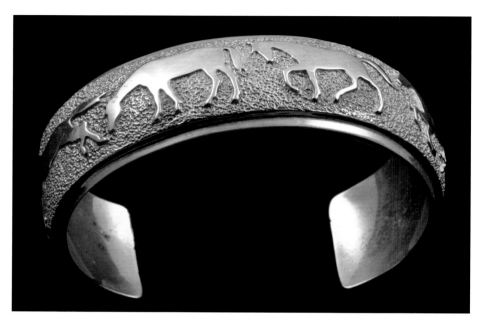

Silver cuff with signature horses design by Northern Cheyenne jeweler and former congressman Ben Nighthorse Campbell, c. 2000. Private Collection.

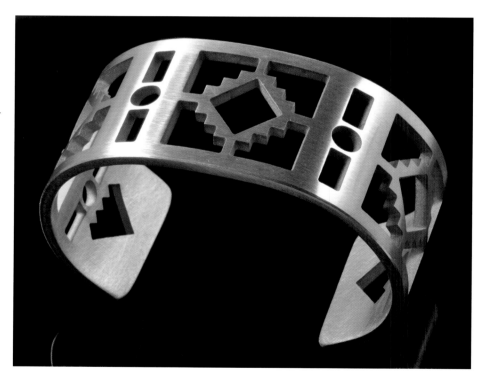

Cutout stainless steel cuff with rain and lightning imagery by Carlton Jamon, Zuni, 2014. Private Collection.

A decade of bracelet designs by Orville Tsinnie, 2002–12. Author's Collection.

"restorative return" that invests Native artists with collective creative strength.

Lately, concerns have been expressed by collectors and dealers about the future of Indian arts collecting, and whether the younger generations are as interested in acquisition as those who have come before them. Technology has altered many consumer patterns. Attendance at the main Indian arts shows remains brisk, but the future is still unclear. A number of artists have banded together to create cooperatives, collaborations, and possible alternative markets to ensure sales; these ventures are too new to evaluate. It may be safe to say, however, that Native Style is likely to keep consumers intrigued since fashion's appeal is always timeless.

We can ask more immediately: what is the future of the Indian bracelet? To find the answers, it never hurts to consult those artists who are currently recasting Indian jewelry into something even more durable for the future.

Liz Wallace, known for her technical expertise and knowledge of antique Indian arts, responded immediately: "More freedom of design, for sure. Artists are more empowered and connected to clients and the world now, and we can call our own shots. I'm very excited!"

J.T. Willie, a lively designer with a key role in today's Navajo Arts and Crafts Enterprise, attempts to clarify: "My definition of Native Style is what you see every day from modern designers such as Tom Ford, Louis Vuitton, Prada, and how we transform that art form into Native— as Natives adding our own taste because of reaching out to the traditional designs and linking them to modern forms."

Wayne Nez Gaussoin, an activist for Native Style, added his perspective as someone who also teaches jewelry-making to young Natives: "Lately, I've chosen to design with a lot of found objects and repurposing materials in my work. As a metalsmith, I feel it's important not only to pay attention to the aesthetics of a given piece of work, but also to the materials used."

Someone who has worked hard to bring a fresh and increasingly influential aesthetic to his art work is Pat Pruitt, and to him we leave the last word. Taking a moment to think at his busy 2012 SWAIA Santa Fe Indian Market booth, Pruitt summed up his belief in the future of the Indian bracelet with a concise one-word statement: "Unrelenting!"

This young artist of the future has unlimited design possibilities open to her.

CHAPTER EIGHT

DESIGN AESTHETICS IN THE COLLECTING OF BRACELETS

There is a powerful connection between design and personal preference. Bracelets have attracted more collectors than all the other jewelry forms combined. Getting collectors to explain their passions isn't easy work, but pride in personal bracelets shines out at Indian arts shows and other gatherings. The cuff shape has had a great deal to do with inspiring both makers and buyers. We have also seen that fashion casts a compelling spell on such artistic creations.

Some collectors still point to specific individual artists as their inspiration. If that artist has been successfully articulate about the magic a great bracelet brings its wearer, he or she develops a loyal following. As previously described, master jeweler Charles Loloma certainly set the bar for such a performance: he had a way of getting potential purchasers to feel that his bracelet was *meant* for them. Friendships between artists and collectors have created some remarkable cuffs, a reminder that art patronage is historical and international in its scope.

What does this mean for twenty-first century collecting of Southwestern Indian bracelets? The influence of the Internet looms large, particularly through dealer and artist websites and the powerful eBay auction site. Many aspects of collecting remain super-competitive, since the antique historical and high-end markets contain limited quantities of desired objects. In particular, Indian-made bracelets are very collectible. Vintage nostalgia and appreciation for older

designs has even made adornment from the 1960s through 1980s increase in demand and value. Nowadays, traditional venues like flea markets and antique shows may not easily yield quality items. Estate sales and auction sales tend to contain more worthwhile goods.

Travelers to the American Southwest have the best market for collecting at hand, but even this region has shrunk in terms of reputable outlets. Often a collection is born from a successful purchase. As always, buying from the Native maker is the best way to go, but these opportunities may be limited to established Indian arts fairs and markets. The annual SWAIA Indian Market in Santa Fe and the Heard Museum Guild

Ernie Lister, master silversmith and antiques dealer, knows his art history.

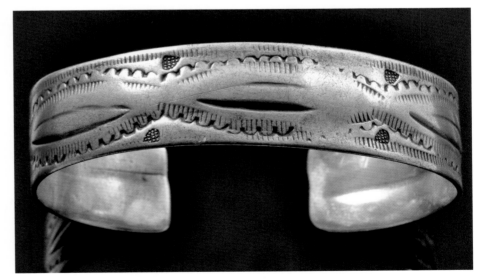

This late nineteenth-century Pueblo band shows signs of wear; while it indicates its original owner wore it frequently, such a condition can lower its value in the market.

The author drove through a blinding rainstorm to purchase this fine bangle by Terry Leonard at the Zuni Art Show in 1995.

Fair and Indian Market are two of the best places for buying directly, although prices can and will be high.

Many collectors use dealers they trust and enter into close relationships with these sellers and the Indian artists they work with. Ethical buying and selling practices are essential, since there is a very real black market of forgeries and reproductions. Nor does it hurt to remind would-be collectors that even digital photographs and measurements can sometimes be misleading.

This means that collecting, as always, is a matter of following an individual's heart. Not only must the design appeal to the buyer, but the bracelet needs to fit comfortably. The scale of a cuff's size

Hopi overlay bracelet with Mimbres rabbit design by Bueford and Dina Dawahoya, c. 1990. Author's Collection.

is another consideration point. Body size does contribute to the collector's perceptions of which bracelets he or she chooses. Artists, past and present, make bracelets with human scale in mind. Many cuffs maintain a "masculine" appearance, while more delicate bangles are created for feminine wear. Some collectors "type" tribal styles: Navajo bracelets are seen as predominantly masculine pieces; the clean contrasts of overlay chosen by Hopi smiths can be considered unisex; and Zuni bracelets often are constructed on a small scale meant for people of petite stature.

Collectors of Southwestern Indian bracelets fall into various categories. There are collectors whose interest in a piece stops if it's made after 1930. Other collectors prefer "traditional" bracelets made between 1920 and 1960, including cluster styles that were most popular with Native wearers. Another category of collector chooses bracelets on the basis of the quality and type of turquoise set on the cuff. Fads and fashions influence those who collect vintage bracelets, especially items from the Fred Harvey tourist era. High-end collectors who don't choose antique bracelets look for pieces made by a select group of living (or recently deceased) artists who use gold and other fine materials. A stampede occurs in the marketplace when a Charles Loloma, Kenneth Begay, Julian Lovato, or Joe H. Quintana bracelet surfaces for sale.

Many individuals, however, come to Indian bracelet collecting without preconceived notions. In most cases, they are embracing the mystique of the cuff, the maker's heritage, and the personal enhancement that item gives the wearer. Southwestern Indian design, however, usually is the "glue" that binds, and that glue leads to personal discoveries that make collecting enjoyable. Countless

books for collectors offer the adage that one should "buy what you like." While true, collecting bracelets can also be a financial investment. A good bracelet is going to cost more than adornment like rings and earrings.

Therefore, it pays for a collector to develop criteria for collecting that will bring the most satisfaction. There is no one definition for what a Southwestern Native-made bracelet should look like. Nowadays, they run the gamut from plain silver to richly complex designs that may not even look ethnic in any respect. Becoming an educated consumer always works, along with developing relationships with artists and dealers who will be helpful. The more one looks at Indian-made jewelry, the more one learns. Even looking at jewelry where the quality varies helps the collector to learn visual nuances.

Relationships based on trust with those who deal in this jewelry are essential. For collectors starting out, this means

learning why you want your dealer to be an ATADA or IACA member, or why shopping at a museum gift shop enables you to make safe purchases. A reliable dealer will look out for your interests once he or she knows what they are. Dealers often act as the representatives of specific artists and serve as a middleman between the maker and the buyer. The author remembers in her first years as a collector finding a Hopi-made bracelet with a Mimbres rabbit design. The bracelet didn't fit her, but dealer Steve Simpson (at Twin Rocks Trading, Utah) contacted the husband and wife team Bueford and Dina Dawahoya, and arranged for them to make a cuff with the same design that did fit.

One last concern in a world that has become irrevocably wired: be wary of sales photos, whether on eBay or the Internet. Even good photographers can make pictures of jewelry and bracelets that don't tell the whole story. There is

What Indian Market sellout artist's wife is known for her proudly worn display of multiple bracelets by her spouse?

no comparison to looking at the physical object. This is a collecting world where, if you establish a good, trusting relationship with a dealer or artist, you are in a better position than relying on a photograph.

For those looking for historic or vintage bracelets, estate sales and auctions in regions outside the Southwest have been good sources in recent years. Those looking for older jewelry do best in the Southwest by attending the New Mexico antiques shows held in August, or visiting Santa Fe, Albuquerque, and Scottsdale.

Guilty or Innocent? Two cuffs that might be backroom fakes from a reservation border town.

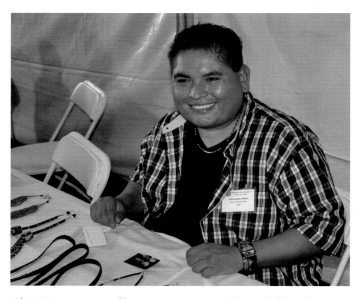
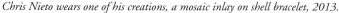

Chris Nieto wears one of his creations, a mosaic inlay on shell bracelet, 2013.

Makers and buyers enjoy the excitement of the annual SWAIA Santa Fe Indian Market.

Some of the most knowledgeable dealers in older Indian jewelry reside outside the Southwest, but they can usually be found at the main antiques shows in Arizona, California, and New Mexico. Gallup is not the place to look for older jewelry, although pieces from the end of the vintage era surface there on occasion.

Bracelets are much more personal statements than other jewelry forms. They get noticed by others, and many who don bracelets report that they provide the wearer with a sense of completion. Collectors should also note that there is a large Southwestern Style market for pieces made by non-Native smiths; these are the sort of works one may find in a magazine like *Cowboys and Indians*. The advantage to staying with Native-made cuffs lies in the fact that such an item is fashioned with a guaranteed cultural integrity in design and outlook. If the piece is an older one, it represents history and social context. We choose objects to live with because they please us and become meaningful. What can be better than a piece of living art that is truly Americana?

And, as an educator, the author asks that enthusiasts and collectors keep an eye on the young Native artists who have begun showing at markets and having their work on display in museum shops and galleries. Investing in the living is one way to do our part in society. If you come to love this jewelry and prize your bracelets as objects of desire, revel in adding to a young person's career development. There's a certain pleasure in standing at an artist's booth at an Indian arts show with friends and acquaintances, and thinking to yourself, "Look at so-and-so's work now. I remember when he/she was just starting out…"

Developing a sense of design aesthetics is personally enriching. You grow as a collector by sharpening your visual senses, understanding the relationship between material, shape, texture, and meaning, and choosing adornment that enhances personal identity. Becoming a connoisseur is something that shouldn't be restricted to the privileged few. Any chance to grow our critical thinking and aesthetic judgment makes us stronger intellectually and spiritually.

American Indian design, when executed freely and purposefully, has a way of going to our hearts. Collectors help make Southwestern Indian bracelets a living art by celebrating a proud legacy with continuing economic support. Buy Native—design derived from tradition, talent, and individual flair. In other words, this is American art at its finest.

A collector's dream come true: "A Perry Shorty Treasure Chest" of bracelets and rings from the early 1990s. Courtesy of Bill and Minnie Malone.

Because metalwork techniques tell us so much about pre-1970 bracelets, a brief glossary of terms is added here. Collectors and students of Indian jewelry-making benefit from understanding key processes and tools.

ANNEALING:
Process in which metal is heated and cooled to make it more malleable; relieves stresses on metal that occur during earlier shaping, bending, or rolling.

APPLIQUÉ:
Decorative technique in which a cutout design is fastened onto the metal by soldering.

AWL:
A pointed tool of iron or steel used to punch holes or incise surfaces, as in engraving; one of the oldest tools for decorative marking when used jointly with files.

BEZEL:
A metallic vertical box or housing into which a stone can be mounted and tapped into place.

CARINATION:
A shape used on older bracelets consisting of a triangular cross-section that comes to a point, or apex, away from the wrist, thus forming a keeled or carinated ridge. Created by casting the piece in a V-grooved mold.

CAST, CASTING:
Process for shaping metal by pouring molten metal into a mold carved or shaped to a desired form or design; once the metal has cooled, it is removed from the mold and unneeded pieces are cut or filed away. Other forms of casting include tufa casting, cuttlefish casting, and lost-wax casting.

COLD CHISEL:
A chisel shaped and tempered to chip, cut, and decorate cold metal; used by early Native smiths up to the 1880s and revived regularly afterwards.

DIES:
The early nineteenth-century die was a rod made from discarded pieces of iron with a decorative form at one end; a later type of die is a metal form into which silver is pressed.

EMBOSSING:
A process that creates relief decoration through the raising of a metal surface by striking the piece from the back, popular from the 1880s through 1920s; embossed bracelets are made using a combination of male and female concha and button dies.

ENGRAVING: Involves the scratching of shallow lines or other tracks into a metal surface; rocker engraving is done by rocking a short-bladed chisel corner to corner while pushing forward.

FABRICATION: Process of assembling a bracelet out of its various **components, e.g., materials,** techniques, and design. ·

FILEWORK: A form of surface decoration used to create repetitive groove marking, enhance raised details and other effects. Filework ranges in shape from round to triangular.

INGOT: Metal cast into a block for storage; this metal came from U.S. and Mexican silver coins that were heated, melted, and poured into sand or volcanic stone molds to cool. Most early coin silver was made by the ingot process, but its use decreased after 1930 when silver slugs and sheet silver were introduced. Contemporary smiths can and do revive this process when making old-style jewelry. The ingot silver process has also been used by those attempting to make fakes of older pieces.

INLAY: A design technique in which colored material, like shell or semiprecious stone, is glued onto a metal base.

MANDREL: A tool used to bend and round metal bands into cuff shapes.

OVERLAY: A technique used by Pueblo jewelers, and now used by all jewelers, but notably Hopi smiths, in which a design is cut, using a jeweler's saw on a flat piece of metal and then sweat soldered onto a piece of the same size through a special heating process; recessed areas are oxidized or blackened to contrast with the highly polished top piece.

OXIDATION: A natural or artificial process whereby silver is darkened or blackened.

PUNCHES: Angled pointed tools that apply decoration to a metal surface when hammered; this process is known as *chasing*. The punch is moved across metal in a steady motion.

REPOUSSÉ: A technique of creating decoration in relief form, in which the back of a bracelet is hammered or pushed through to create raised, domed, or embossed designs known informally as "bump-ups."

SANDCAST: Casting done by pouring molten metal into a vessel filled with firmly packed sand shaped into desired design; back of a sandcast piece is flat but can have interesting texture.

STAMPING, STAMPS: Act of hammering or punching a relief pattern onto a metal sheet to use as a design element.

SWEDGING: Technique used to produce a bracelet of ridged silver grooved on both surface and backside, developed as early as 1850 and much revived afterwards.

TUFA: A specific form of soft volcanic ash, or pumice, found in abundance around the Navajo reservation, and particularly in the Ganado, Arizona, area. Tufa is lightweight and can be carved into molds for casting silver.

WROUGHT: This means only hand tools were used to create the piece; hand-wrought bracelets can be beaten, hammered, or twisted.

VALUATION

Southwestern Indian jewelry has a number of price ranges depending on the nature of the work involved. There is an inexpensive commercial and craft market, which can be riddled with fraudulent imports and questionable materials. An affordable middle range exists for much vintage era and handmade jewelry fashioned by Native artists. Antique pre-1930 jewelry and high-end contemporary art wear command expensive price tags. In the years preceding 2015, silver and gold prices rose to sticker shock levels for both makers and buyers. Semi-precious stones, both traditional and newly mined and adopted, have also risen in price.

Those entering the lower end of the Indian arts marketplace may still obtain a silver bracelet for $100 to $150, depending on how much stone work is used. Pieces between $150 and $350 may be more reasonable to expect. The middle-range cost level for genuine Native-made bracelets, fairly newly made, run between $350 and $1,200, as of mid-2014. Expect to pay double (and even triple) this range if you purchase a heavy-gauge silver or gold cuff. The market price for such bands depends on four key factors: materials, quality of technical execution, quality of design, and who made the piece. A high-end bracelet by a contemporary fine artist jeweler will start at four figures—and can easily run to five figures. A random look at late 2013 prices for high-end bracelets reveals amounts like $3,200, $5,700, and $27,000.

For those who seek historic era and vintage bracelets, price will be affected by the piece's age, its provenance (that is, who owned it after it was made), physical condition, and general appeal to collectors.

Names do resonate in these markets, and makers' names and hallmarks become more commonly known after 1930. Bracelets made before 1930, and those fashioned later by master innovators, are likely to be the most expensive due to their limited supply in the marketplace. The January 2014 issue of the *Indian Trader* reported on a December 9, 2013, auction at Bonham's San Francisco: one of the notable sales that day was a Charles Loloma bracelet that fetched a $27,500 bid. Collectors eagerly seek pieces that come on the market through estate sales and auctions, especially if their previous owner was a well-known collector or dealer. Do not be shocked by prices in excess of $10,000 to $18,000.

Vintage bracelets, including commercial pieces from the Fred Harvey tourist era, have risen steadily in price over the past decade; this also includes works from the 1970s, a decade that had previously been regarded suspiciously by collectors. A tourist era bracelet can be quite affordable, sometimes offered under or around $200. Those who eagerly scour antique shows and flea markets around the United States will be less likely these days to make "finds" since this category of collectible has such demand. Be sure to check eBay to see a good approximation of the prices asked for vintage (1930–1980) bracelets. The sustained entrance of global players to the ethnic art marketplace over the last twenty years has had its effect, too. Savvy collectors from Japan and Europe keep a sharp eye on the market and forge mutually beneficial deals with artists and dealers.

Collecting Indian-made bracelets means understanding certain conditions attached to older objects. Such pieces may have repurposed or replaced stones or decoration taken from concha belt plaques or pins. Turquoise taken from the regional U.S. mines is a collectible with historic overtones, and bracelets set with such stones retail for thousands of dollars. Because this living art has an active black market, it's best to work with reputable shop owners and dealers, especially those who have membership in ATADA and IACA and are therefore bound by ethical considerations.

Since today's Southwestern Indian bracelets are made by canny artists who operate in competition with other Native artists and mainstream jewelry designers, expect to find that everyone has a strong sense of their worth in the market. Buying directly from a Native jeweler is the safest option, but do not make the mistake of attempting to bargain down the price of one of that person's creations—those days are long gone. If you wish to commission a piece by an artist, expect to pay some money up front to ensure the transaction, secure an invoice, and mutually agree on when this work will be completed. In some instances, things may work better if you pursue a commission via the artist's gallery representative.

Southwestern Indian bracelets are a highly satisfying collectible, and the new collector will soon gain a sense of how the Indian arts market runs at its own pace. While specific Native wear, like squash blossom necklaces and concha belts, may be out of favor at the moment, there is *always* a demand for bracelets. The old adage "buy what you like" has never been more meaningful. We now have a global society where diversity is prized, especially from cultures with a profound sense of aesthetic beauty,

RESOURCES FOR RESEARCH

Being an informed consumer is the best recourse for the would-be collector. Southwestern American Indian jewelry has a shadowy black market located in the Pacific Rim, in Mexico, and in basement workshops in reservation border towns. The neophyte collector needs to understand how fakes, forgeries, and reproductions can easily masquerade as the genuine article. The antique Indian jewelry market, which includes historic era and vintage bracelets, is limited in quantity and highly competitive. While there is more vintage period jewelry available for sale and the demand for contemporary bracelets remains strong, the variety of work involved can appear bewildering.

Educating yourself in a specific decorative art involves two steps. The first step requires reading as much reliable literature on the subject as possible, especially those books and articles written by scholars, museum professionals, cultural historians, jewelry experts, and Native artists themselves. Consult the *Bibliography and Works Cited* section in this book. The author's 2001 publication, *Southwest Silver Jewelry* is still perceived as one of the best resources for identifying antique and vintage Indian jewelry forms up to 1970. If you want excellent information on contemporary fine art jewelry, investigate works by Dexter Cirillo and Diana Pardue. Martha Hopkins Struever's authoritative study of Charles Loloma is enhanced by her long friendship with the artist. Books by Mark Bahti, Robert Bauver, and Lois Dubin are also reliable guides. Other works cited in the Bibliography provide a scholarly listing of key publications for the study of Southwestern Indian jewelry-making.

The second step necessitates looking extensively at the jewelry itself and spending a lot of time physically examining pieces. This means visiting museums, Indian arts markets including the big ones in Santa Fe and Phoenix, antique shows and other selling venues, reputable shops, trading posts, and collectors' holdings when the opportunity arises. Even looking at specious or jewelry of dubious provenance helps to reveal inadequacies. Talk to other collectors and seek out experts with questions, if you have them.

Online research can be very helpful. The major museums with good permanent collections of Southwestern Indian jewelry, including bracelets, often have websites with collection information. Here are some of the most important locations:

National Museum of the American Indian, Washington, D.C. and New York
www.nmai.si.edu

Eiteljorg Museum of American Indians and Western Art, Indianapolis, IN
www.eiteljorg.org

Heard Museum, Phoenix, AZ
www.heard.org

Institute of American Indian Arts (IAIA), Santa Fe, NM
www.iaia.edu/museum/

Millicent Rogers Museum, Taos, NM
www.millicentrogers.org

Museum of Indian Arts and Culture, Santa Fe, NM
www.indianartsandculture.org

Museum of Northern Arizona, Flagstaff, AZ
www.musnaz.org

Wheelwright Museum, Santa Fe, NM
www.wheelwright.org

Organizations that provide assistance with buying, selling, provenance, and misrepresentation issues include the following:

Antique Tribal Art Dealers Association
www.atada.org

Indian Arts and Crafts Association (IACA)
www.iaca.org

Indian Arts and Crafts Board, Washington D.C. (IACB)
www.iacb.doi.gov

The author's blog, on Indian arts and collecting in Indian Country www.southwesternsouvenirs.com

Commercial sites exist in great numbers, and people have their favorites. These sites range from trading posts that act as art galleries or historical resources, galleries in urban settings, and dealers who maintain inventories and sell Indian arts via the Internet. Two sites, marked by experience in the business, are very different in nature.

The first is the website for Twin Rocks Trading Post in Bluff, Utah, which features high-quality merchandise and excellent background information by top-notch writers. The second resource is maintained by Wright's Indian Arts in Albuquerque, New Mexico; a monthly survey of this site offers an impressive visual view of fine goods, including bracelets, that have recently reached the market. The informed consumer should and will research and locate his or her own preferences.

BIBLIOGRAPHY AND WORKS CITED

Adair, John. *The Navajo and Pueblo Silversmiths*. Norman: University of Oklahoma Press, 1944.

Arrow Novelty Co., Inc. *Catalogue of Indian Design Silver Jewelry*. New York: n.p., 1912 [1987 facsimile reprint].

Bailey, Garrick and Roberta Glenn Bailey. *A History of the Navajos: The Reservation Years*. Santa Fe: School of American Research, 1986.

Bahti, Mark. *Silver + Stone: Profiles of American Indian Jewelers*. Tucson: Rio Nuevo Press, 2007.

Bahti, Tom. *Southwestern Indian Ceremonials*. Flagstaff: KC Publications, 1970 (1982).

Batkin, Jonathan. *The Native American Curio Trade in New Mexico*. Santa Fe: The Wheelwright Museum of the American Indian, 2008.

Bauver, Robert. *Navajo and Pueblo Earrings 1850-1945; Collected by Robert V. Gallegos*. Los Ranchos de Albuquerque: Rio Grande Books, 2007.

Baxter, Paula A. "Cross-Cultural Controversies in the Design of American Indian Jewellery." *Journal of Design History* (U.K.) 7, 4 (Winter 1994): 233–245.

————. *The Encyclopedia of Native American Jewelry*. Phoenix: Oryx, 2000.

————. "Native North American Arts: Tourist Art" In *The Dictionary of Art*, edited by Jane Turner. London: Grove, 1996, vol. 22, pp. 667–670.

————. "Navajo and Pueblo Jewelry, 1940-1970: Three Decades of Innovative Design Revisited." *American Indian Art Magazine* 21, 4 (Autumn 1996): 34–43.

————. "Nineteenth Century Navajo and Pueblo Silver Jewelry." *The Magazine Antiques* 153, 1 (January 1998): 206–215.

————. *Southwestern Indian Rings*. Atglen, PA: Schiffer Publishing Ltd., 2011.

————. *Southwest Silver Jewelry*. Atglen, PA: Schiffer Publishing Ltd., 2001.

Bedinger, Margery. *Indian Silver: Navajo and Pueblo Jewelers*. Albuquerque: University of New Mexico Press, 1973.

Bell, Barbara and Ed Bell. *Zuni: The Art and the People*. 3 vols. Grants, NM: Squaw Bell Traders, 1975–77.

Black, J. Anderson. *A History of Jewelry: Five Thousand Years*. New York: Park Lane; dist. by Crown, 1981.

Bird, Allison. *Heart of the Dragonfly*. Albuquerque: Avanyu Publishing, 1992.

Branson, Oscar T. *Indian Jewelry Making*. 2 vols. Tucson: Treasure Chest, 1977.

Bsumek, Erika Marie. *Indian-Made: Navajo Culture in the Marketplace, 1868–1940*. Lawrence: University Press of Kansas, 2008.

The C.G. Wallace Collection of American Indian Art, November 14, 15, and 16, 1975. Auction sales catalogue. New York: Sotheby Parke-Bernet, 1975.

Cirillo, Dexter. "Design Motifs in Southwestern Indian Jewelry." *American Indian Art Magazine* 34, 4 (Autumn 2009): 58–69.

————. "Off the Cuff: Just Bracelets." *Native Peoples* 22, 5 (September/October 2009): 40–47.

————. *Southwestern Indian Jewelry*. New York: Abbeville Press, 1992.

————. *Southwestern Indian Jewelry: Crafting New Traditions*. New York: Rizzoli International Publications, 2008.

Coe, Ralph T. *Lost and Found Traditions: Native American Art, 1965-1985*. Seattle: University of Washington Press, in assoc. with American Federation of Arts, 1986.

Collecting Native America: 1870-1960. Edited by Shepard Krech and Barbara A. Hail. Washington, D.C.: Smithsonian Institution Press, 1999.

Colton, Mary-Russell F. "Hopi Silversmithing—Its Background and Future." *Plateau* 12 (July 1939): 1–7.

Diaz, Rosemary. "Thinking Outside the Cube: Jeweler Cody Sanderson." *Native Peoples* 22, 1 (Jan.–Feb. 2009): 34-36.

Douglas, Frederic and Rene D'Harnoncourt. *Indian Art of the United States*. Exhibition catalog. New York: Museum of Modern Art, 1941.

Dubin, Lois Sherr. *The History of Beads: From 30,000 B.C. to the Present*. Revised and expanded edition. New York: Abrams, 2009.

————. *Jesse Monongya: Opal Bears and Lapis Skies*. New York: Hudson Hills Press, 2002.

————. *North American Indian Jewelry and Adornment: From Prehistory to the Present*. New York: Abrams, 1999.

————. "Northwest Meets Southwest: A Mission of Sharing." *Native Peoples* (May-June 2001): 2–6.

Dubin, Margaret. *Native America Collected: The Culture of an Art World*. Albuquerque: University of New Mexico Press, 2001.

Dye, Victoria E. *All Aboard for Santa Fe: Railway Promotion of the Southwest, 1890s to 1930s*. Albuquerque: University of New Mexico Press, 2005.

Engber, Daniel. "Who Made That? (Redskins Logo)." *The New York Times Magazine* (November 17, 2013), 21.

Ewers, John Canfield. "The Emergence of the Named Indian Artist in the American West." *American Indian Art Magazine* 6 (1981): 52–62, 77.

Farnham, Emily. "Decorative Design in Indian Jewelry." *Design* 35 (March 1934): 13–15, 23–24.

Frank, Larry with Millard Holbrook II. *Indian Silver Jewelry of the Southwest 1868-1930*. West Chester, PA: Schiffer Publishing, 1990.

Gaussoin, Wayne Nez. Personal Communication. March 2014.

Gay, Peter. *Art and Act: On Causes in History—Manet, Gropius, Mondrian.* New York: Harper & Row, 1976.

Gopnik, Blake. "Americana Redux: The New Magic of Vintage Ralph Lauren." *Newsweek*, November 19, 2012: 65–6.

Hait, Pam. "The New Look in Indian Jewelry." Collector's Edition. *Arizona Highways* 55, 4 (April 1979): 1–46.

Harvey, Brian, E.W. Jernigan, and Gary Witherspoon. *White Metal Universe: Navajo Silver from the Fred Harvey Collection.* Exhibition catalog. Phoenix: Heard Museum, 1981.

Hatcher, Evelyn P. *Visual Metaphors: A Methodological Study in Visual Communication.* Albuquerque: University of New Mexico Press, (1974) 1989.

Heard Museum Library. Native American Artists Resource Collection.

Heard Museum Library. Pamphlet Files and Vertical Files.

Hill, Gertrude. "The Art of the Navajo Silversmith." *The Kiva* 2, 5 (February 1937): 17–20.

Hougart, Bille. *The Little Book of Marks on Southwestern Silver: Silversmiths, Designers, Guilds and Traders.* Washington, D.C.: TBR International, 2011. Updated and expanded, 2014.

Hunt, Walter Ben. *Indian Silversmithing.* New York: Bruce Publishing, 1960.

Hutchinson, Elizabeth. *The Indian Craze: Primitivism, Modernism, and Transculturation in American Art, 1890-1915.* Durham and London: Duke University Press, 2009.

Indian Arts and Crafts Association and Council for Indigenous Arts and Culture. *Collecting Authentic Indian Arts and Crafts; Traditional Works of the Southwest.* Summertown, TN: Book Publishing Company, 1999.

Jacka, Jerry. "Innovations in Southwestern Indian Jewelry: Fine Art in the 1980s." *American Indian Art Magazine* 9 (Spring 1984): 28–37.

Jacka, Lois. *Navajo Jewelry: A Legacy of Silver and Stone.* Flagstaff, AZ: Northland Publishing, 1995.

Jernigan, E.W. *Jewelry of the Prehistoric Southwest.* Santa Fe: School of American Research, 1978.

King, Dale Stuart. *Indian Silverwork of the Southwest.* Vol. 2. Tucson: Dale Stuart King, 1976.

Kirk, Ruth Falkenburg. *Southwestern Indian Jewelry.* [Reprinted from *El Palacio*.] School of American Research, Papers, no. 38. Santa Fe: School of American Research, 1945.

Loscher, Trica and Diana F. Pardue. "Humor in American Indian Jewelry." *American Indian Art Magazine* 34 (Autumn 2009), 50–57.

Lowry, Joe Dan, and Joe P. Lowry. *Turquoise Unearthed: An Illustrated Guide.* Tucson: Rio Nuevo Press, 2002.

Lowry, Joe Dan, and Joe P. Lowry. *Turquoise: The World Story of a Fascinating Gemstone.* Layton, UT: Gibbs Smith, 2010.

Lund, Marsha. *Indian Jewelry: Fact & Fantasy.* Boulder: Paladin Press, 1976.

Mangum, Richard and Sherry Mangum. "The Hopi Silver Project of the Museum of Northern Arizona." *Plateau* n.s., no. 1 (1995): complete issue.

Martin, Ned and Jody, and Robert Bauver. *Bridles of the Americas. Vol. 1. Indian Silver.* Nicasio, CA: Hawkhill Press, 2010.

Matthews, Washington. "Navajo Silversmiths." *Second Annual Report to the Smithsonian Institution from the Bureau of Ethnology, 1880–81.* Washington, D.C.: Government Printing Office, 1883, pp. 167–178.

————. "The Night Chant: A Navaho Ceremony." *Memoirs of the American Museum of Natural History* 6 (1902).

McGreevy, S.B. "Indian Jewelry of the Southwest: Finished In Beauty." *Art and Antiques* 3 (May–June 1980): 110-117.

McLerran, Jennifer. *A New Deal for Native Art: Indian Arts and Federal Policy 1933–1943.* Tucson: University of Arizona Press, 2009.

Mera, H.P. *Indian Silverwork of the Southwest.* Vol. 1. Tucson: Dale Stuart King, 1960.

Miller, Shari Watson. "Patania: 70 Years of Excellence, Part 1 of 2." In *Modern Silver Magazine* 2001. www.modernsilver.com/patania.htm

Mills, George. "Art: An Introduction to Qualitative Anthropology." In *Art and Aesthetics in Primitive Societies.* New York: Dutton, 1971, pp. 73–98.

Monongye, Preston. "The New Indian Jewelry Art of the Southwest." *Arizona Highways* 47 (June 1972): 6–11, 46–47.

Monthan, Guy, and Doris Monthan. *Art and Indian Individualists.* Flagstaff: Northland Press, 1975.

Moore, J.B. *Illustrated Catalogue of Navajo Hand-Made Silverwork.* Chilocoo, OK: Indian Print Shop, 1906.

Neumann, David L. "Navajo Silverwork." *El Palacio* 32, 7-8 (February 1932): 102–108.

Ostler, James, Marian Rodee, and Milford Nahohai. *Zuni, A Village of Silversmiths.* Zuni: A:shiwi Publishing, 1996.

Pardue, Diana. *Contemporary Southwestern Jewelry.* Layton, UT: Gibbs Smith, 2007.

———. *The Cutting Edge: Contemporary Native American Jewelry and Metalwork.* Phoenix: Heard Museum, 1997.

———. "Everything is Golden." *Native Peoples* 25, 1 (Jan.–Feb. 2012): 36-40.

Parsons, Elsie Clews. *Pueblo Indian Religion.* 2 vol. Lincoln: University of Nebraska Press, 1939, 1966.

Prown, Jules David. "The Truth of Material Culture: History or Fiction?" In *History from Things: Essays on Material Culture.* Washington, D.C.: Smithsonian Institution Press, 1993, pp. 1–19.

Pruitt, Pat. Personal Communication. August 2012.

Ringlero, Aleta. M. "Man of Steel: Innovative Pueblo Jeweler Pat Pruitt." *American Indian Magazine (NMAI)* Summer 2008: 18–21.

Robbins, Catherine C. *All Indians Do Not Live in Teepees (or Casinos).* Lincoln: University of Nebraska Press, 2011.

Rosnek, Carl and Joseph Stacey. *Skystone and Silver: The Collector's Book of Southwest Indian Jewelry.* Englewood Cliffs, NJ: Prentice-Hall, 1976.

Rushing, W. Jackson. *Native American Art and the New York Avant-Garde.* Austin: University of Texas Press, 1995.

Sandner, Donald. *Navaho Symbols of Healing: A Jungian Exploration of Ritual, Image & Medicine.* Rochester, VT: Healing Arts Press, 1979 (1991).

Schiffer, Nancy. *Jewelry by Southwest American Indians: Evolving Designs.* West Chester, PA: Schiffer Publishing, 1990.

———. *Masters of Contemporary Indian Jewelry.* Atglen, PA: Schiffer Publishing, 2009.

Sei, Toshio. *Knifewing and Rainbow Man in Zuni Jewelry.* Atglen, PA: Schiffer Publishing Ltd., 2010.

Sides, Hampton. *Blood and Thunder: An Epic of the American West.* New York: Doubleday, 2006.

Slaney, Deborah C. *Blue Gem, White Metal: Carvings and Jewelry from the C.G. Wallace Collection.* Phoenix: Heard Museum, 1998.

Stacey, Joseph. *Arizona Highways Turquoise Blue Book.* Indian Jewelry Digest from Arizona Highways Collector Series. 1975.

Struever, Martha Hopkins. *Loloma: Beauty Is His Name.* Exhibition catalog. Santa Fe: Wheelwright Museum of the American Indian, 2005.

Survivance: Narratives of Native Presence. Edited by Gerald Vizenor. Lincoln: University of Nebraska Press, 2008.

Tanner, Clara Lee. "Southwestern Indian Gold Jewelry." *The Kiva* 50, 4 (1985): 201–218.

Tisdale, Shelby J. *Fine Indian Jewelry of the Southwest: The Millicent Rogers Museum Collection.* Santa Fe: Museum of New Mexico Press, in assoc. with the Millicent Rogers Museum, 2006.

Torres-Nez, John. *Beesh Ligaii in Balance: The Besser Collection of Navajo and Pueblo Silverwork.* Santa Fe: Museum of Indian Arts and Culture, 2004.

Totems to Turquoise: Native North American Jewelry Arts of the Northwest and Southwest. Kari Chalker, general editor. Exhibition catalog. New York: Abrams. in assoc. with American Museum of Natural History, 2004.

Turnbaugh, William A. and Sarah P. *Indian Jewelry of the American Southwest*. West Chester, PA: Schiffer Publishing Ltd, 1988.

Tyler, Hamilton A. *Pueblo Animals and Myths*. Norman, OK: University of Oklahoma Press, 1975.

Von Neumann, Robert. *The Design and Creation of Jewelry*. 3rd edition. Radnor, PA: Chilton Book Company, 1982.

Wallace, Liz. Personal communication. Feb. 2013.

Willie, J.T. Personal Communication. March 2014.

Wright, Barton. *Hallmarks of the Southwest*. Revised and expanded edition. Atglen, PA: Schiffer Publishing, 2000.

Wright, Margaret Nickelson. *Hopi Silver: The History and Hallmarks of Hopi Silversmithing*. Albuquerque: University of New Mexico Press, 1998 (2003).

Zeitner, Jane Culp. *Gem and Lapidary Materials for Cutters, Collectors, and Jewelers*. Tucson: Geoscience Press, 1996.

INDEX